W9-CBD-156

Ball Control Offense
and Disciplined Defense
in Basketball

Ron Van Ryswyk

Basketball Coach
Frostburg State College

Parker Publishing Company, Inc.

West Nyack, N.Y.

© 1967 BY

PARKER PUBLISHING COMPANY, INC.

WEST NYACK, N.Y.

ALL RIGHTS RESERVED. NO PART OF THIS
BOOK MAY BE REPRODUCED IN ANY FORM OR
BY ANY MEANS, WITHOUT PERMISSION IN
WRITING FROM THE PUBLISHER

LIBRARY OF CONGRESS
CATALOG CARD NUMBER: 67-13000

PRINTED IN THE UNITED STATES OF AMERICA

BC

To my Mother,
Beulah Elizabeth
The Benevolent Perfectionist
and
To the dedicated players
with whom and from whom
I have learned the game

A Word from

the Author

I like to win. I want to win them all. I want every "fair advantage" possible. There are basically two ways to realize winning. The first is to have, year in and year out, superior player material. This means recruiting, which I have never been in a position to do. I'm not sure I'd enjoy it if I could recruit. According to certain research, one study of my own included, those coaches who do recruit list it as one of the undesirable tasks in their work. A coach who expects to have superior material regularly in the absence of recruiting is speculating on the most remote fringes of statistical probability.

The second way to increase the probability of success is to do a superior job of coaching. Superior coaching means teaching boys to play the game well. Coaching should be exactly this.

The main theme of this book, however, is how to take coaching one step beyond teaching boys to play well. Human limitations being what they are, at some certain point boys can make no further adjustments toward perfection. The only avenue to improvement is to adjust and manipulate the game (within the letter and spirit of the rules) to the boys.

It is my contention that average or "marginal" athletes cannot operate with perfect success, using the same methods and techniques used by All-Americans. Their need is for sound, disciplined training in every possible aspect of the game, for they have not been endowed with any superior "innate" skill on which they can rely to provide the winning margin.

There is, in my opinion, a most effective way to do nearly everything in basketball. The well-coached player will have enjoyed the guidance and aid of his coach in all aspects of the game. In brief, there needs to be more effective attention (coaching) given to both the boy and the game. It then becomes unlikely that anything during a game or season will come as a surprise to the player. He will have been prepared. Of course, there are aspects of the game for which I have no suggestions. For these areas, they are "on their own." My attitude, if unique, is unique in degree. How much of the time is the player free to do as "whim" directs? Not often, say I.

The usual remark is that this is "ultra-conservatism," evident in some coaches of past eras—the eras of set plays and 10-8 scores. Not so. I'd describe it as Disciplined Progressivism. This type of game is not slow, not "restricted" in the strict sense of the word. I want action and I want it *now*, I want it *fast* and I want it *continuously*. I don't want any mistakes so "Boys, do it the way you were taught."

Winning basketball results from *not* making mistakes. It follows therefore, that when mistakes occur, they should be explainable. No theory guarantees perfection. The tested strategies in this book, however, very definitely guarantee a high degree of success probability—in that they will *minimize errors,* and it will certainly follow that, other things being equal, more games will be won than lost.

If your players are not superior these ideas hold promise. They are usable and have been tested at all levels from junior high through college, in boys' and even girls' competition.

In 12 years of coaching I have never had a team that averaged six feet or more; this period includes six years of coaching at college level. Ball control offense and effective man-to-man defense has, in spite of this size limitation, resulted in a record of above .700 since 1951. Based on my experience, I am certain that coaches from junior high through college can employ these ideas with success. And coaches and managers of recreational leagues, church leagues, etc. will also find a variety of helpful hints in the material presented here.

The graduating college physical education major and/or basketball theory class student will learn things of value, too. There is no basketball textbook available that completely serves his need. All too often, books used for the coaching student are refined coaches' notebooks, mixtures of accumulated ideas, some of which have been tested, some merely theory. Some volumes are superfluous and non-integrated into a unified, organized scheme. An effective book on basketball should include at least one solid, sound system complete in every detail on all aspects of play with "all the fat trimmed off," i.e., no filler or extras. The coach has a desperate need to know what is essential and "what ain't." Time is always, in the end, the critical determinant of teaching success. To this end, only the necessary items should be stressed. In addition (and in this way perhaps a bonus is included), there is a crying need for exact detail in teaching the essentials. What exactly does the coach say in selling an idea to the players? What are the reasons given by the coach as he talks and shows players that they need to do it his way; what words, examples, demonstrations, warnings, etc. can be produced to convince the player that this *is* the best way, that this way is foolproof for us? This book will provide both suggestions and examples of proven methods used to answer these and other questions which confront every basketball coach.

Some feel that basketball is on unsound ground when too many rules for action appear, when too-strict an atmosphere prevails. This is possible and I find a safeguard that usually saves me from such a fate. If a player develops suppressed behavior it will vanish momentarily whenever the coach discontinues teaching or stops continuing to stress a particular guiding rule. The suppression occurs only during the learning phase of the rules; once the rules are learned, *really* learned, reaction within the rule is automatic and accomplished instinctively.

To sum up this introductory section, my experience has convinced me that the most reliable key to success with players who aren't the tallest and the most highly skilled is the type of basketball based upon the following tenets:

1. Continuity pattern offenses, highly disciplined to work for and to get the "good" shot. This implies a 5 man attack, 5 men moving, 5 men combining efforts to cause one defender to falter.

2. Good ball handling.
3. *Consistent* free throw shooting.
4. Highly disciplined man-to-man defense with constant hustle and few fouls.
5. Dedicated boys possessing strong character capable of developing a high degree of self-discipline and team discipline. This means a burning desire to pay the price—and they'll be basketball players before they graduate.

One of two teams is going to win, it may as well be ours.

Contents

Part I
Ball Control Offense

ONE

Ball Control

and Pattern Play

The good shot

In one way we're particular about the kind of shots we get in a game. We are so choosey that we'll often pass up all opportunity to score until we get exactly the kind of shot we're after. We want the "good shot." We have a few concrete, simple rules that guide each and every player as to whether a shot can be taken. *All* shots must be good shots.

The Good Shot guidelines are as follows: 1) the shooter *sincerely believes* he can make the basket. He cannot fire away and *expect* to make a few and miss a few. If a shooter misses, I sincerely expect *him* to be surprised. If he expects to miss he shouldn't shoot. The shot must also be "his shot," a shot from one of the certain spots or situations that are his favorite ones. 2) He must be in *balance* (comfortable, "feel good," in complete control of his shooting equipment—whatever that includes). He cannot be hurried. This does not prevent the fall-away shot or discourage the wrong-foot jumper, etc., for all boys but it does for some. If the wrist and hand have complete support and control, okay; this

3

varies with the boy and each boy can learn to recognize his own limitations. On the other hand, some lay-ups are bad shots because the boy is off balance, and even though the shot is a six inch shot it shouldn't be taken because the probability of missing is too great and we don't want to surrender the ball to defensive rebounders. 3) There must be offensive rebounders *available* (not necessarily already in position) that will enable us to match the number of their rebounders to within one man. *Example:* I don't shoot if I'm one against two opponents who are in better rebound positions than am I. I will shoot if I'm one-on-one, or two-on-two, three-on-three, etc.—and if the first two guidelines apply. Of course we will always go for the unmolested lay-up, as this is one on nothing.

In addition to these three guides our game strategy dictates the distance limits of our shots. Our usual plan is to take all lay-ups and jumpers up to fifteen feet. Sometimes we decide, before a half or during time out, that we take only the un-molested lay-ups. Sometimes we agree we're going to fire the thing as soon as we get close enough to see it, providing the guidelines, 1) *think* we can score and 2) in balance and not hurried—much!, apply. In these cases we will sometimes not wait for rebound support.

Dependence of ball control on the good shot

Courage is required to play control basketball. Many coaches will admit that it makes sense to "hang on" to the ball until the ideal shooting opportunity presents itself. It is something else again to condition boys to actually do so in game situations. One must be convinced that sooner or later, the good shot opportunity will occur, or more exactly, that the offensive team can cause it to occur.

Ball control means not only waiting for the ideal situation and instant to shoot, it most certainly means not losing the ball via violations, offensive fouls or error commitment such as allowing interceptions, steals, etc. In brief, we may wait two and one-half minutes before we take a shot. We may make 20 passes, move five men 15 different times, or pass up six mediocre opportunities to shoot. We are convinced the opponents cannot interrupt this plan, i.e., they cannot intercept our passes, they cannot prevent our player movement (cuts, screens, etc.). Ball control does not guarantee that we will not lose the ball before we score, but it nearly does!

Ball control and pattern play

We believe the best way to control the ball offensively is to operate in a pattern. Most teams "play a pattern." How much of a pattern? How many players are involved? How much of the time do they pattern? How effectively do they "Pattern"?

Five-man patterns seem to hold the most promise. Some coaches say basketball is a two-man game. Feed a buddy and screen for him as he shoots, the third and fourth men rebound as the fifth balances for defense. Some patterns such as two-man-plus occasionally invite the third man into the play, to feed a teammate and screen for a different teammate who will accept the feed for a shot.

I don't like the idea—and I've used it for several years—because it means that Sam and Joe are playing this time; Jack, Chuck, and Dave are not in it, at least for scoring. Too often offensive play is dominated by one, two, or three men because the others know full well that their lot is to perform flunky duty. This concept does not bother me, the coach, but it would take several angels with well-tuned harps to convince me that the players aren't affected. I prefer that each and everyone of the five men be charged with being a potential contributor to *all* phases of the game which includes scoring. I am not for an instant suggesting that all men can score equally well, but I insist that they have considerable opportunity to do so. I'll take five men with 15 points each rather than with two with 40 each. Furthermore, when I personally play, I have no respect or regard for a teammate who feels he must or may shoot for me. This argument in favor of five-man patterns is one that has as its essence team morale, or spirit, or whatever you will. Nothing, no nothing, is as important as spirit. Nothing!

A second reason for holding to five-man patterns is one of mathematical logic. Five men moving at once, according to a single over-all concept, all ultimately becoming potential scorers, are more apt to succeed against the defense than is an attack of four or fewer men.

Having now stated the case for five-man patterns, the general term "pattern" itself should be defined. A pattern is a unified plan of action which is designed to create a problem for the opponent, namely a situation which will cause perhaps only one defensive man to falter, at which instant the offensive team (hopefully) can score. Patterns can cause problems for the offensive patterning team as well; indeed this is often exactly the case. Our boys know better how to "get out of trouble" than the opponents if for no reason other than our familiarity with it! Sometimes we say, in half jest, "Here is the pattern, use it and it'll create the problem; you solve the problem!"

Need for pattern

If you are the better team, you should win without need for a pattern. If you have a much weaker team you may well lose in spite of an excellent pattern. If you have able players with ability to shake off defenders and get free for a shot and if these men are also good shooters, you don't necessarily need a pattern.

If, however, teams are fairly evenly matched, good pattern play is my choice. If you are behind in the game, you most definitely need to do two things: 1) score, 2) prevent your opponents from using the ball to increase the lead. A good pattern will produce good shots—which you now need. What you don't need is a greater tendency to bang away—chances are you'll miss more and fall further behind. If you are ahead in the score, you don't need to release the ball and you don't even need, relatively speaking, to score. You should work for only the sure shots which will insure that you stay in the lead. Nothing pleases me more than to see my front-running opponent fire away promiscuously—because it means we at least have a chance to get the ball!

Meaning and importance of discipline in offense

To play patterned ball control there must be discipline. Not discipline as punishment, but discipline as it implies order and self-control. Each player must, first and foremost, be *unselfish*. He must be as eager to see a teammate score as he is to score himself. He must have courage to overcome the temptation to break pattern and go "lone-wolfing." He must have *faith* in the pattern, faith that opportunities to score will come just as surely as the sun will rise tomorrow. He must have *temper* control and keep his composure and poise, particularly when he is behind, at a disadvantage or the underdog. These several factors can be *taught* and they can be *learned*. The coach who cannot teach them should probably play free lance, not pattern, basketball.

Boys who are disciplined, who execute a good pattern and who play ball control are not going to lose many games to teams of near equal ability.

Values and advantages of disciplined pattern ball control

Playing a ball control offense enables the offensive team to shoot the shot they desire instead of firing away under dictates of the defensive team. It also minimizes the chances that the ball will be lost, without a shot, to the defense. In order that these two results be realized, we believe the system should: 1) be fast, not slow as some "set-play" teams played in bygone days. 2) be continuous; it should never stop or even hesitate and give the defense a chance to relax or study the offensive plan. 3) create problems for the defense, e.g., it should cause them to become tired, confused, screened, etc. 4) be fun and enjoyable to the players who execute it. 5) be pleasing to the observer or fan. 6) be a system with a low failure probability. Each of these factors is an advantage and each supports the others.

What ball control is not!

The most frequent single criticism of ball control basketball is that the players are "afraid to shoot" or that they make "fifteen passes and shoot ... maybe!" Ball control may be an apologetic, unsure theory built on fear of failure—or it can be just the opposite. We believe that ball control is built on confidence, aggression, cool logic and proof or evidence of success (history) in past games. In order that one might subscribe to this latter belief, one must first have it as a basic philosophy. As Carl Sandburg in *Washington Monument by Night* remarks, "nothing happens unless it is first a dream." Yes, first believe that execution of ball control is certain to result in successful point-making. It is for this very reason that we believe it to be superior.

Offensive scoring opportunities will arise that can be exploited immediately and directly without recourse to pattern. These situations are not passed by—we don't run three screens to get a lay-up if it isn't necessary. Ball control does not restrict or reject the easy chances to score.

Blending ball control offense with defense

When defensive resistance of the opponent is greatest, so is the need for ball control. Inversely, free lance play owes much of its success, if not most of it, to an assumption that the opponent will not be defensively tough. Should that hope prove warranted, free lance has my support—in part. Believe it or not, many leagues or areas seem to operate within the mystical unwritten code that "none of us will perfect our defense—let's keep it a fertile ground for free lance play." Apply sound and solid defense, specifically the proud and sound man-to-man brand, and I see trouble for free lance play. Sending boys into battle against the heavy armament of well-coached man-to-man defense with only the side arms of free lance offense is similar to the situation which Tennyson vividly describes, here in paraphrase:

> All in the valley of death
> ... cannon to the right of them
> cannon to the left of them,
> cannon in front of them ...
> Into the jaws of death
> Into the mouth of hell
> Rode the free-lancers!

By that comparison I suggest ball control is the best weapon versus solid defenses. One can conclude thereby that a solid defense on the part of the team that employs offensive ball control makes the best and most formidable total game. We mean, in other words, that it would indeed be as foolish to play a careful, deliberate ball control offense and score, for example a meager 45 points, as to play a lackadaisical porous defense and allow the offense to score with little resistance. Certainly, sound defense must accompany the concept of ball control offense. Ball control *defense* then is part of ball control offense. In summary, *total* ball control is controlling the ball on defense as well as offense.

Blending ball control to free throw shooting

In addition to striving for high percentage field goal shooting as we have already discussed, some consideration must be given foul shots. Ball control teams will get a relatively high number of chances to win it at the foul line. This is because they will handle the ball more and probably draw more funds from the defense. In addition, it has already been determined that sound, solid defense will be played by this same ball control team. Good defense implies: 1) prevention of the opposition scoring and, at the same time, 2) not fouling. Therefore a complete ball control game will usually get more free throw attempts than another team because it (a) is on offense more and being fouled, (b) is better disciplined to foul infrequently while on defense.

How this is done is discussed in appropriate places later in this text.

Needless to say, it behooves this type of team to be highly efficient free throw shooters. This skill can be learned to considerable extent. These points are described in Chapter 18.

The need for two games, screen and free lance

For reasons I cannot fully explain, some opponents are very good defensively versus free lance play but can be screened and patterned, or more accurately, you must screen them or you'll never shake them off to get the good shot. We usually find that the best drilled man-to-man defenses must be attacked with a screen game. The simple fundamentals (one-on-one isolation, give-go, etc.) or free lance moves, will not disturb their defense.

SCREEN GAME RESEMBLES A PASSING GAME

The best screen games appear to be a passing offense. This does not mean that there is no such thing as a screen game based on dribbling. More possibilities exist in a passing type screen game with resultant greater rewards than with considerable dribbling. Screen games are fully discussed in the next chapter. The passing screen game threatens more opponents more frequently than any other type screen game. We believe that we dare not start into a season without a solid, basic screen game.

TIME REQUIREMENTS OF A SCREEN GAME

We find that a good screen game takes or requires about five to six weeks to learn (well). Therefore we start the first day of practice so that it is ready or nearly ready by the opening game.

This is the approximate time for a green squad or for a squad which is being introduced to the screen game for the first time. They can *run* a screen game after a few sessions, but it achieves maturity and high efficiency only after about six weeks.

VALUES OF FREE LANCE GAME

Some teams can't be screened. Some referees won't allow "our" screens. Some teams don't need to be screened—one can score quicker and easier with free lance moves. Sometimes a free lance game is a necessary variation from one's screen game. The different tempo or "look" of the free lance operation changes the pitch of the game. It must be a mistake not to have some kind of free lance system in the offensive bag of tricks.

FREE LANCING FROM THE PATTERN GAME

The free lance game that best complements a good screen pattern game is perhaps to free lance from the same floor alignment as the pattern game. In this way it looks as though a team is attempting to pattern, yet the concentration is to do whatever we can without pre-assignment. We try to build into our basic screen game a lot of free lance opportunities. These will be included as we proceed through the following pages.

TWO

The Trample Offense

> Oh what a tangled web we weave
> when first we practice to deceive.
>
> *Sir Walter Scott*

There are surely as many ideas on offense as there are coaches who coach plus fans who observe. Anyone who buys a ticket to a basketball game is nearly as close to the action as is the bench coach. Many of these fans are full of ideas. Any coach may "invent" an offensive plan, only to see it in use three years later a few or a hundred miles away. Too many coaches for too many years have developed too many ideas for the "inventor" to stand much of a chance to be really creative.

We have experimented with many, many ideas in fifteen years. Some of these, we thought were "our own," only to discover them in use elsewhere. Some ideas presented herewith we believe to be the products of our own thinking and experience and they truly are, *but,* other coaches doing *nearly* the same thing who achieve nation-wide fame may seem to deserve credit. We merely attempt to expound on what we've done, what we've used, what we've developed (a product of borrowing, adapting, altering) as the kind of game we like and believe in.

Shuffle concepts

We were raised in an area of the Midwest where the Oklahoma Shuffle had—and probably still has—considerable influence on

11

some coaches. We continue to like some of the basic shuffle ideas, namely: (1) pass instead of dribble, (2) get the ball close to the basket by passing, (3) bring the players later *without* the ball (it's easier that way!), (4) bring the players to the basket and to the ball from the rear of the defense, or from the side away from the ball (this prevents the defense from keeping both men and ball in view), (5) keep the pattern continuous, constantly moving without need to "stop and re-set," (6) keep all or most of the players alternating in a planned sequence of options to get a chance to score, (7) move players constantly to other positions on the floor, (8) considerable use of screens, (9) good floor balance (most of the time), (10) threats are not all of the same type (some moves are lateral, some are vertical in, some vertical out, some are post, etc.).

Other favorite strategies

We've used some shuffle ideas for years. I like the high and low post game. I like the single guard alignment as opposed to the two-man front. I like the vertical post moves (post men screening down and up the lane). I like the twin post idea. I like all ten of the shuffle concepts listed previously. Put these all together and my favorite offense takes the appearance of Diagram 1.

We call this game our Twin Post Trample or "Trample" for short. Trample: "to domineer harshly over; to put, force, reduce." [1]

The Trample, how it works

We line the middle guard directly in the center of the court. He is usually ready to begin operations about two or three strides above the free throw circle.

Each wingman (or forward) begins approximately on the free throw line extended. One wing we call "W" or "weakside," the other we call "S" or "strongside." These two players do not determine their own status; they are weak or strong depending upon which side "P," the high post, assumes his position. If P posts the right side as in Diagram 1, the right wing is strongside and vice versa if P posts left.

"L" or low post always sets on the same side as does P.

---

[1] *American College Dictionary.* Random House, New York, 1962.

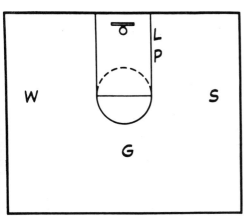

Diagram 1

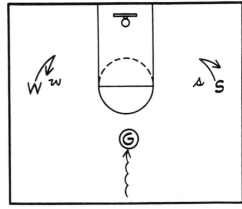

Diagram 2

In this Twin Post Trample we try to do one of two things, namely play (1) weakside which we also give the number "22" or (2) strongside, "23."

We prefer to play 22 or weakside and will do so whenever we can.

As soon as G approaches within three steps of the key top, *both* S and W begin to "jockey" for freedom from defensive men s and w. This is a two step maneuver, Diagram 2. S and W are facing the lane as they start to jockey. They step toward the basket by taking a long first step with their baseline foot, to the rear or baseline side of the defensive man, Diagram 3. This step is followed by a long crossover step with the other foot (foot nearest the time lane), Diagram 4. If at this time the defensive man has not retreated with this "dummy play" maneuver, the wingman raises a hand and signals for the feed from G and continues on to the basket for the "back door" or dummy play easy basket, Diagram 5.

Diagram 3

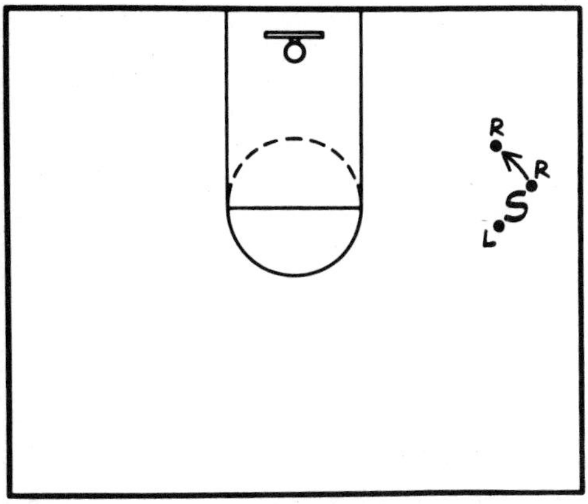

Diagram 4

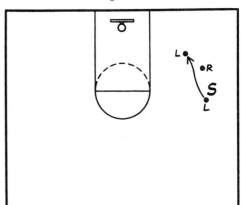

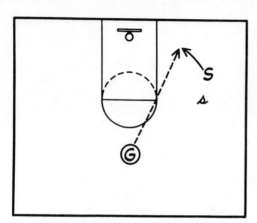

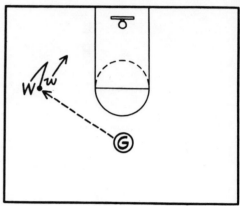

| Diagram 5 | Diagram 6 |

We want both S and W to jockey even though we will always feed W, if possible. Should W be well defended, we always have a possible outlet to S, following this S feed with our strongside options.

It is imperative that S and W start to jockey *before* G is ready to feed as we want them to be free *at* the time G picks up his dribble, not sometime later!

Assuming that W successfully frees himself, the feed will be an overhead two hand pass from G to W at a point about six feet in from the sideline and on the free throw line extended. See Diagram 6.

We like the two hand overhead pass and use it almost exclusively. We can move the ball *over* defenses quite effectively. This keeps the ball in shooting position almost constantly and this insures good ball control by keeping *two* hands on the ball most of the time. Occasionally if the defensive play is tight, we will use a bounce pass that comes up a step to the outside of S or W.

| Diagram 7 | Diagram 8 |

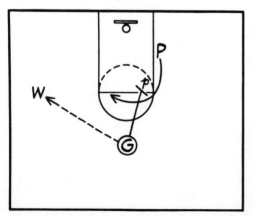

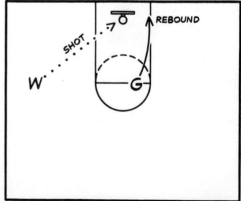

As soon as the ball leaves G's hand, all four empty men (men without the ball) *move*.

ASSIGNMENTS FOR WEAKSIDE 22

The movement route rules are:

G feeds W and goes away from the ball by cutting down the lane, screening for P who comes up the lane on the strongside (which is the side containing the most offensive men) to meet G, Diagram 7.

This action enables G to be an effective screener on defensive p. If W shoots quickly, G continues down to rebound the appropriate corner of the board, Diagram 8.

In these latter cases, S has vacated the wing spot and G then fills this position and becomes the new right wing.

If G sees no quick shot by W (usually there will not be one) he then looks for L (low post) coming high outside the lane and tries to screen defensive 1 with a front screen. This means that G has two screening assignments on the weakside play, first for P, then for L. Many times P has gone to the ball side before G can be useful as a screener, or defensive p is not "screen-able." In this case G abandons this screen assignment and hunts for defensive 1, which is a more critically essential screen. If we find that G can get a good screen for P and that he is able to hold p for a length of time that destroys the second screen (on 1) we then have to tell G to either not screen p, but go directly for 1 down the outside of the lane, *or* keep the screen on p and forget about 1. Usually we find G working on 1 most of the time and with the most rewarding results, Diagram 9.

Rule for S when ball goes weakside

S starts toward basket and at L (low post). At a point about half way to L's original position, L and S should meet because L began to move at the same instant as did S (*everyone* moves when the ball moves, except possibly the ball handler W).

S tries to walk his defender into the body of L which is the most effective of all screens, a rear screen, Diagram 10. We tell *both* S and L that it is *your* job to see that defensive s is screened; don't wait for each other!

If S is successful in flashing to the basket without molestation

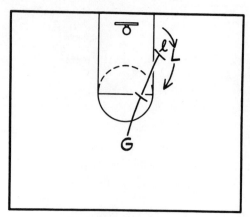

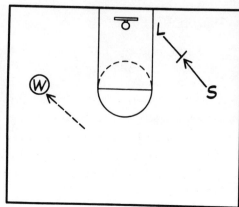

Diagram 9   Diagram 10

from s, W feeds him on our favorite scoring move, the "come-under" or S coming under the basket. S can go over or under L screen. W tries to deliver the ball about net high, as early as possible—don't permit the pass to be late, unless unavoidable. S should not hurry past the basket as we may feed him late or "out of time" and if we feed him we expect him to score the cross-under lay-up on the side of the basket nearest the feed, Diagram 11.

We insist that this lay-up be a power shot; we want *all* of his body weight to go into the board, a 185 pound shot, if you please. We don't like to run away from this shot or "shoot it on the way by"!

If S isn't open, we do not force the ball in, i.e. pass it into a defensive hornets' nest of hands and *hope* that our boy S hauls it in. We pass up this option and look for the next scoring move. If S is not fed, he stops at the edge of the lane near the basket on the ball side and becomes the new low post, L, Diagram 12.

Diagram 11   Diagram 12

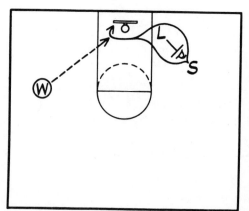

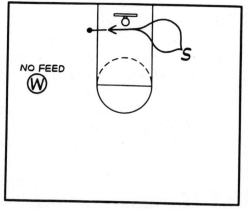

Rules for Low Post L

L screens away from the ball, which will be a back screen on defensive s. L must not set this screen too close as it is then illegal. L must be strong since the defensive s men tend to fight through this screen. The best technique is to keep both forearms across chest or abdomen. L must be trained to look for defensive s, go find him, go to him, otherwise s gets by the screen, Diagram 13.

L holds the screen on s as long as s stays on it or as long as it is effective. When L is no longer an effective s screen, L quickly gets to the top of the lane and his first thought is "hurry to the free throw line and get ready for a two-point free throw," Diagram 14.

In this action L gets set exactly as he would if he had all day to shoot unmolested from the foul line. He faces the basket, gets his feet set, *then* expects the feed. Every boy can make this shot and it counts not one point, but two. W will always look for L at the free throw line if S was not free on the come-under, Diagram 15.

Often L must set up farther back, but he nonetheless gets there *early*, gets ready *early*, before the ball arrives, if possible. We tell L "If we feed you inside the circle, you *will* shoot and you *will* score two!"

If L is not fed, he backs up whatever distance is required to become the new middle guard G, Diagram 16. He must not go nearer W than the exact floor center.

Rules for High Post

The location of P, right or left side, is determined by many factors. If our right wing is left-handed, we often like him to

Diagram 13   **Diagram 14**

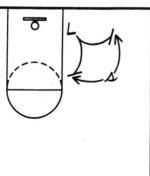
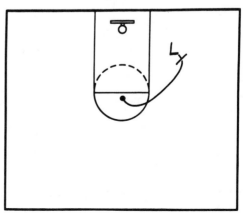

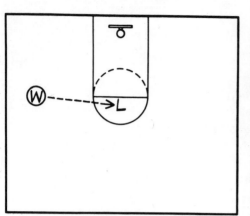

Diagram 15

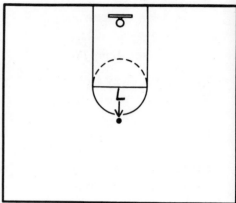

Diagram 16

become strongside so that his cross-under for the lay-up is from the right toward the left; therefore, we would want P to play a right side post—we would feed leftwing W and Trample accordingly, Diagram 17. We do this if our low post L if left-handed which gives him a good move (turning clockwise as he comes up the lane for the two point free throw), Diagram 18.

If our postman, P, is left-handed we slightly prefer that he play right side, Diagram 19.

If our middle guard is a good left-hand driver, we are better aligned with P on the right side for purposes of "clearing-out" W before G feeds, as G brings the ball down this open side for a lay-up attempt, Diagram 20.

Should our left wing be a good baseline driver, we would prefer that he be isolated on the left side and again we would like the strongside to be away from him, Diagram 21.

If our best outside shooter's favorite "spot" is the left wing

Diagram 17

Diagram 18

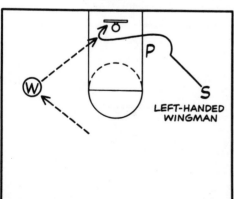

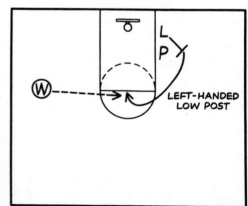

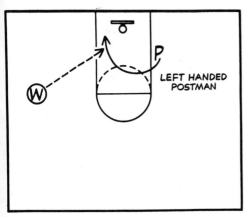

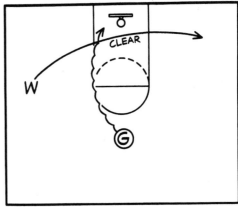

| Diagram 19 | Diagram 20 |

position we would play him there and establish strongside to the right. P is the one who calls the formation and we play in accordance with the placement of our high post, although of course, we may change him over as we come down the floor by command from G or from the bench. If P changes sides, L must do likewise.

We like to get the moving screen of G down the lane and roll the post behind this toward the ball, Diagram 22. Except for this basic move, we tell P that you are basically "on your own" and we are playing a four-man Trample with or without you. Our high post man is free lancing much of the time.

We can feed P at any time; we encourage the feed to P at *any* time in the Trample. As we will demonstrate a little later, our pattern continuity continues in the same way regardless of who has the ball. If, for example, G were to feed P instead, four empty men move as though W had been fed—i.e., we run our "weakside" play, Diagram 23.

| Diagram 21 | Diagram 22 |

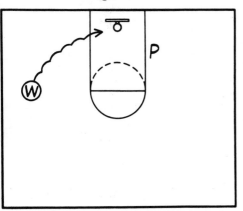

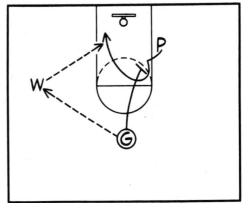

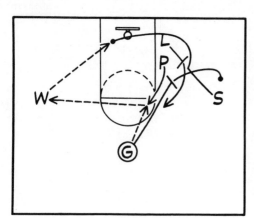

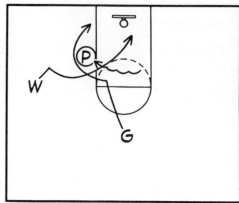

Diagram 23	Diagram 24

We also look for P any time we get into trouble or our pattern bogs down. If our high post man is not an adept scorer, we may use him as a rebounder and run the Trample around him.

We have a general rule that applies to all post men or to any man who becomes a temporary post man, such as a wing man who starts a drive to the basket and is stopped near the lane. This is our Split rule: any time a man has the ball near the lane (post man) and *cannot* or *does* not attempt to score immediately (this usually means he turns away from the basket and faces away) the two nearest men, whoever they are must split (cross over) him! We usually get a shot or give P a chance to relieve himself (feed off), Diagram 24.

The general operational guides for the high post P are: 1) stay away from the ball, then work to the ball. 2) use the vertical-down screen by G if there is one. In executing this assignment, P may start at a medium post, Diagram 25, or high post, Diagram 26, or high inside the circle, Diagram 27, or at a high center post,

Diagram 25	Diagram 26

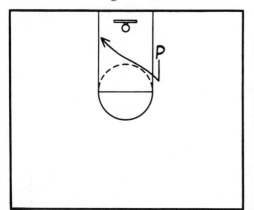

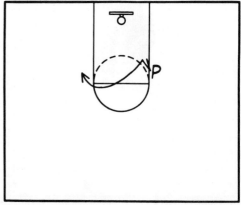

Diagram 28. From these positions he can move directly or indirectly toward the ball as indicated in the diagram. These routes are only suggestive of the freedom he has. P should try to shake his defender and be open as often as possible. The most common mistake P will make is to stand still—he should be constantly on the move unless undefended.

P should operate some in practice from the other four positions. We feel only in this manner will he actually learn the Trample pattern completely. He should have a thorough understanding of the pattern because: 1) he often becomes a feeder if our regular feeders have to seek relief from unusual defensive pressure; 2) he must *not* be in the traffic lanes of our favorite scoring threats as the Trample progresses.

Rules for Weakside W

W jockeys with footwork for freedom from defensive w. Immediately upon reception of the feed from G, he checks his own defensive man. If defensive w is out of position, W drives under or over or set (or jump) shoots. In other words, W scores himself if he can do so with a high degree of certainty.

W next checks for S coming under and if he sees that S might be free, W hangs the ball on the near lower fringe of the strings so that the ball is *there* when S arrives, Diagram 29. W cannot wait until S arrives at the near edge of the lane and then begin the feed, Diagram 30. I do not mean to imply that W will not feed S late because he will, if S is open. It is simply a much easier shot and tougher on the defense to get the ball there early.

If S is defended or if for some other reason W decides not to

Diagram 27	**Diagram 28**

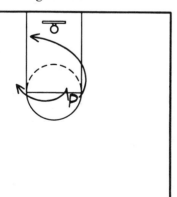 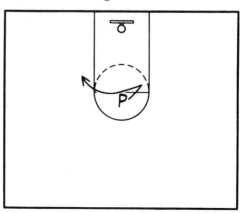

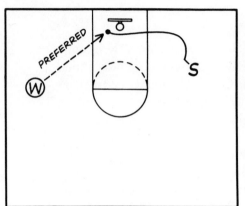

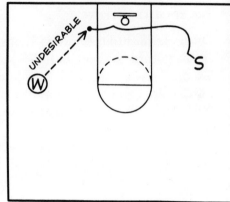

| Diagram 29 | Diagram 30 |

feed and we repeat "Don't force the ball in," W immediately looks for the next option P who has worked for freedom, Diagram 31.

If P is not open W immediately looks for our second favorite option which is L coming up the far lane line, Diagram 32.

Should L not be open immediately W will hesitate just an instant as L retreats one, two, or three steps and then feeds L who has become the new middle guard, G, Diagram 33.

We now have completed the complete cycle of 22 or weakside.

SUMMARY OF 22

In summary, player movement has resulted in these threats which began when the ball moved:

G feeds W, cracks down for P, rebounds a quick shot, screens down on 1, then fades to far side and becomes the new (next) weakside wingman.

| Diagram 31 | Diagram 32 |

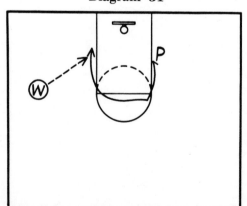

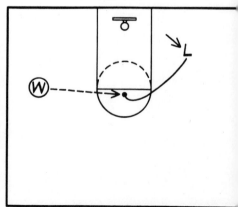

P works toward the ball and stays ball side.

L screens for S, works into G's screen, rolls quickly to the top of the key, retreats and becomes the new middle guard, G.

S walks s into L's rear screen, comes to the ball and stops at the low post on ballside.

W jockeys for freedom, checks his own defense and scores immediately if possible, looks next for S coming under, then for P rolling, immediately for L coming up to the line. The four options, in sequence, are indicated in Diagram 34.

The total pattern 22

The five man action is shown in Diagram 35. The timing is important and will properly govern itself if these guides are kept in mind: 1) The time for all four empty men to move is the instant the ball moves out of G's hand to W. Everyone moves pronto. 2) W must check the four options snap, snap, snap, snap and if none of the four scoring opportunities develop, the ball is *immediately* back to the new G and ready to start the Trample on the opposite side. 3) It helps, in explaining the pattern, to show that the weakside *becomes* the strongside as the four options develop because the strongside men come to the weakside, thus making the weakside the new strongside, Diagram 36. Note, however, that the man with the ball has absolutely nothing to do with this transition since it is the empty men who transform strongside to weakside. W was originally weakside wing but before he returns the ball to G, he has been transformed into S. This explanation aids the learning and avoids confusion in the mind of the learner

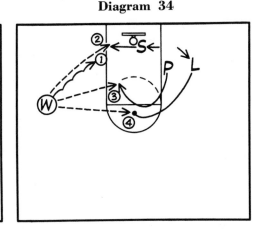

Diagram 33   Diagram 34

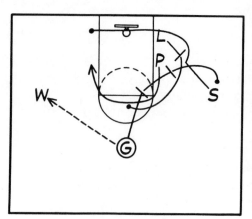

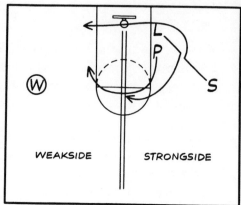

Diagram 35

Diagram 36

as to how he identifies which side is which. Strongside, therefore, is the side on which the two post men are located and it can change as often and as rapidly as the post men can cross the lane.

THE CONTINUITY OF THE TRAMPLE OFFENSE

The four diagrams 37, 38, 39, and 40 show the Trample in complete scheme as it starts left weakside (37), returns (38), then starts right weakside (39) and returns (40). It is now ready to again go left and subsequently return, etc.

EACH MAN PLAYS EACH POSITION

In order to show with complete clarity the sequence of positions played by all men (except the post man, who always plays post), we shall number the men 1, 2, 3, 4, and 5 and have these men retain their numbers throughout the sequence. W is 1, G is 2, S is 3, L is 4, and P is 5, Diagram 41. We shall now go through

Diagram 37

Diagram 38

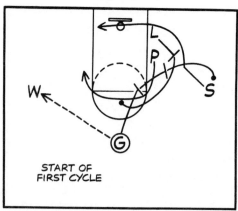

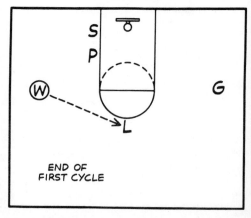

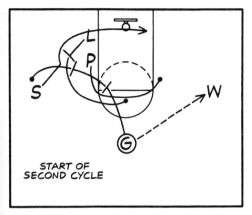

START OF
SECOND CYCLE

Diagram 39

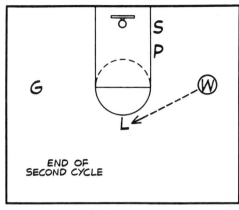

END OF
SECOND CYCLE

Diagram 40

four complete Trample cycles to indicate how each man plays all four perimeter positions and how on the fifth cycle he is back to his original position.

The strongside cycle 23

Why *a Strongside Pattern?*

There are several reasons for the necessity of this attack: 1) We prefer to use 22 weakside, but if defensive pressure prevents our doing so, we need an immediate alternative. 2) Strongside gives a different "look" to the pattern without re-aligning. 3) Strongside complements weakside, i.e., each is a substitute for the other; too much of one leads to educating the defense.

When *to Use Strongside 23*

The *defense* will cue our decision to leave 22 and go to 23.

Diagram 41

Diagram 42

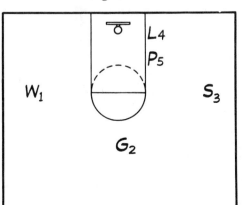

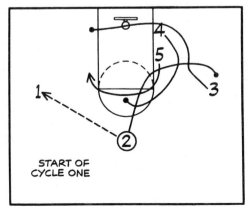

START OF
CYCLE ONE

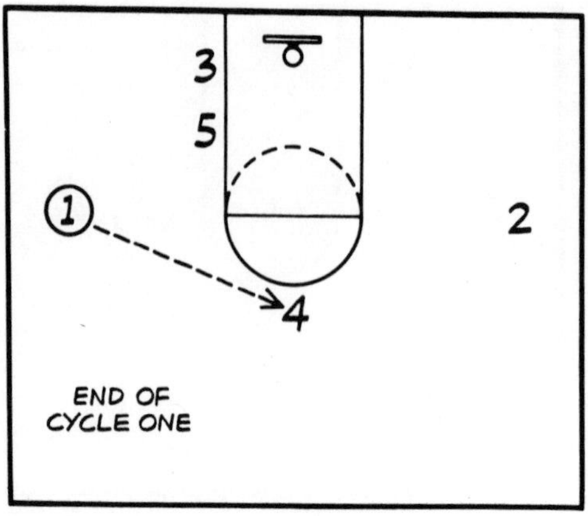

Diagram 43

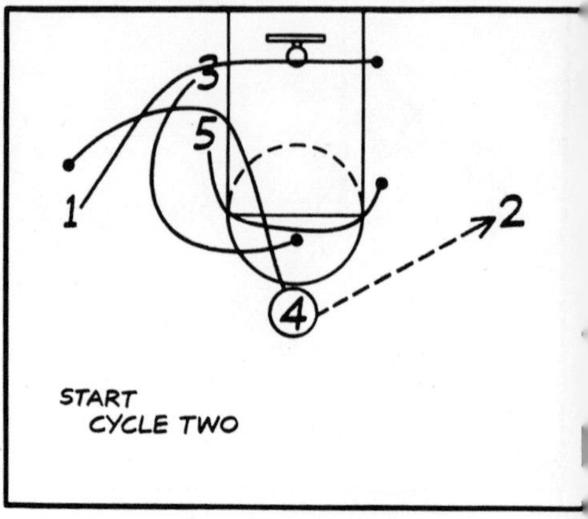

Diagram 44

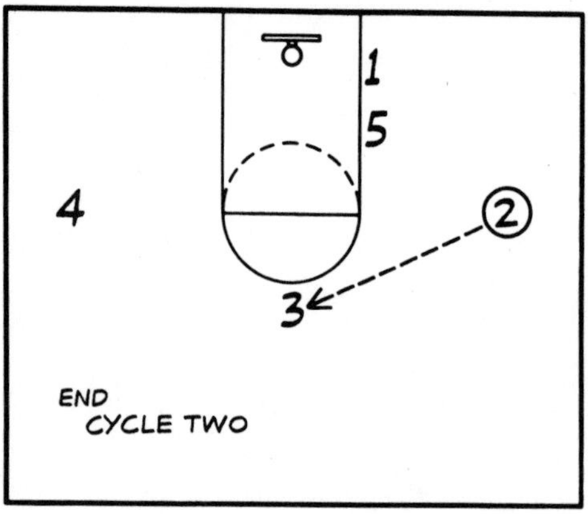

Diagram 45

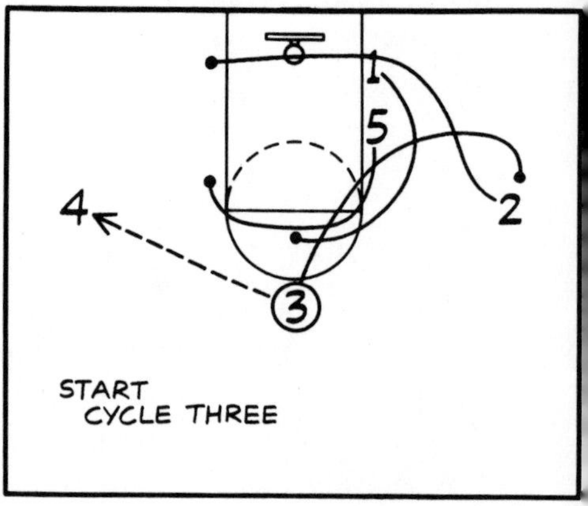

Diagram 46

Diagram 47

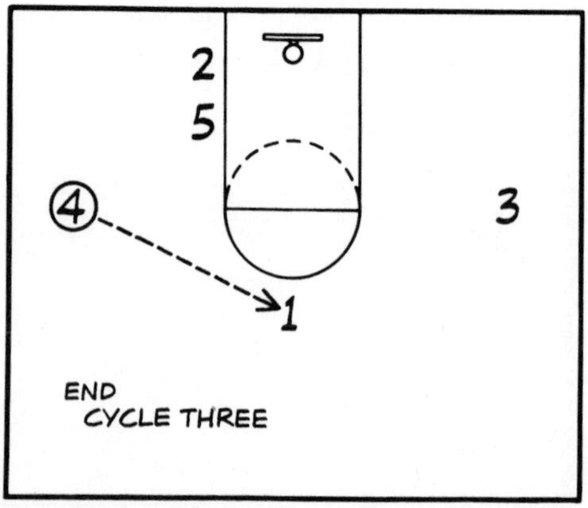

Diagram 48

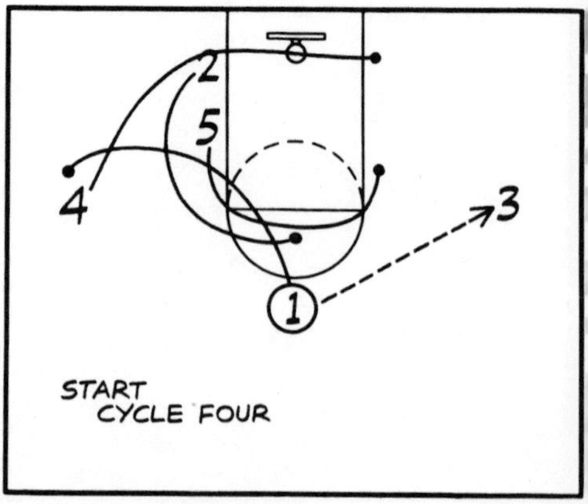

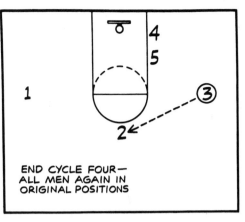

END CYCLE FOUR—
ALL MEN AGAIN IN
ORIGINAL POSITIONS

Diagram 49

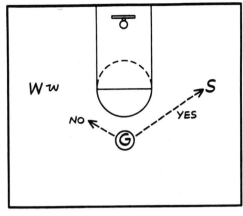

Diagram 50

The specific defensive techniques that call for this change are as follows:

1. If defensive w so efficiently overplays W that G cannot safely feed W, and if W cannot jockey himself free, G will temporarily abandon any intent to go weakside with the ball. G immediately directs his attention to S, Diagram 50.

2. If once having gone weakside and having failed to get the shot, we desire to return the ball from W to the new G, and we find defensive g very effective in his ball side overplay of G, we often decide not to risk the interception and we are ready to play strongside 23, Diagram 51.

3. If we want variety, we may play 23 merely as a change of pace.

Diagram 51

Diagram 52

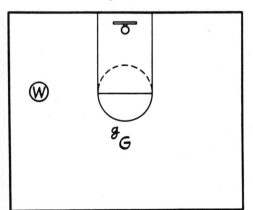

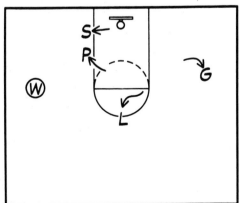

The Strongside Operational Assignments

This variation of the Trample is a take-off from some lessons we learned the hard way in earlier coaching days when confronted by 3-2 zone defenses. The similarity may be noted after having reviewed standardized zone attacks later in the book.

Let us assume that a 22 or weakside cycle was started, W has the ball, S has come to the low post, P has come to the ball, G has cleared away and L has come to the front, Diagram 52.

W has now become S because of the movement of the other players. S decides to run 23. Any signal may be used; we often use the "corner look" or the fake feed to G. If S directs his attention into his own baseline corner, the 23 is on, or if S fakes a feed to G but pulls the ball back in, the 23 pattern is on, Diagram 53.

Here are the assignments:

The man with the ball, S

S looks to his corner; this cue causes L to come to the corner, at least two thirds of the way—or farther if defensive 1 is tight—and immediately turns and faces the lane. We do not want L fed as he comes out, we want him faced in before the feed, Diagram 54. L then becomes the new feeder.

S, after feeding L, runs a direct line give-go at the basket, expecting a return feed—which will often occur—because one minor reason for running 23 was defensive s playing high to prevent a return feed to G.

If S is not fed on the give-go, he continues on through the lane to the far wing position and becomes the new weakside W, Diagram 55.

Diagram 53   **Diagram 54**

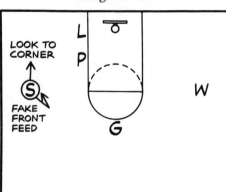

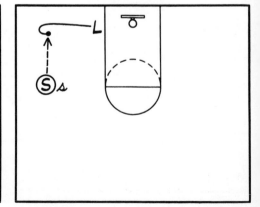

The Post Man, P

P gets the cue that 23 is starting and goes vertically up the lane to rear screen the prime trouble-maker who caused the need for 23, defensive g, Diagram 56. P holds this screen as long as it is effective, then comes fast vertically down the lane on a cut to the basket.

P should not drift closer to the ball than the near edge of the lane because he will have decreased his ability to score, Diagram 57. He will plug up the cutting area of our next cutter. P is the third cutter on 23 (S is first, G is second).

If P is not fed after having cut to the baseline, he quickly returns to his original medium (or high) post position on ball side of the lane, Diagram 58, and awaits the next cycle of 23 or whatever (perhaps 22 will be next).

The middle guard

G waits for P to approach g for the rear screen. As P arrives, G takes a step toward the circle center, which helps walk g into P's rear screen, then breaks fast down the ball side of the lane to the basket. If L in the corner does not feed G, Diagram 59, G stops at the near corner of the board and becomes the new low post, Diagram 60. G has become the second cutter (S was the first one with his give-go move).

The Weakside wingman, W

W rebounds the quick shots and comes out to the new G posi-

Diagram 55

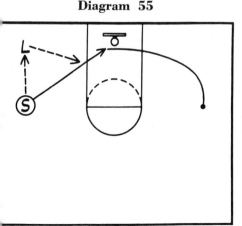

Diagram 56

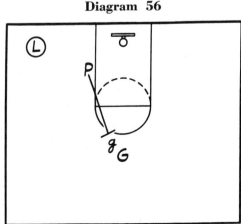

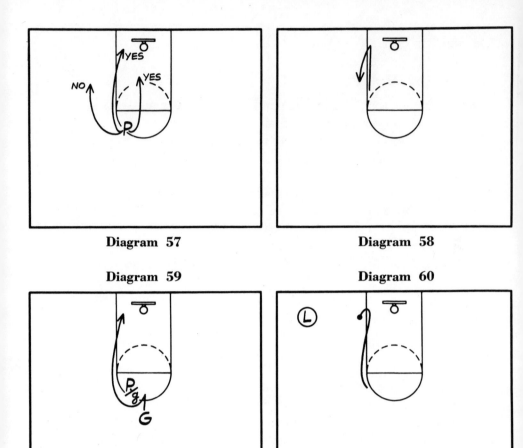

Diagram 57

Diagram 58

Diagram 59

Diagram 60

tion as soon as G leaves on the cut over the post man's screen, Diagram 61.

The cornerman (who was originally L)

L breaks from his low post toward the corner. As soon as he is wide enough to feel free, he turns and faces in. Upon receipt of the feed from S, he likes to feed S on the quick cut. L next tries to score himself by driving the baseline side of 1, as the feed attempt to S will often pull defensive 1 a bit off the baseline, Diagram 62. L next looks for the second cutter G coming hard down the lane. G is usually near edge, but may go middle or far side if defensive g reacts always ball side of P's screen, Diagram 63.

If G cannot be fed, L looks next for the third cutter P.

If all these attempts net no gain, the 23 cycle is nearing com-

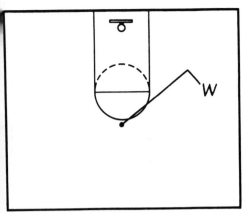

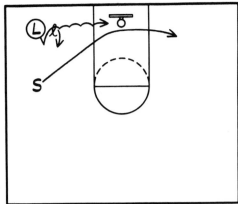

Diagram 61   Diagram 62

pletion. L then dribbles up his sideline and becomes a wingman (new S), Diagram 64.

He may now try to feed the middle guard and run 22, or start a new 23 cycle by asking the new L to come to the corner for the feed.

The total strongside pattern

Diagram 65 indicates the total pattern through one complete cycle.

In summary, the options and their sequence are as follows: S can't feed G, so he feeds L who has come to his corner.

1. cornerman feeds S on the first cut
2. cornerman tries to score himself
3. cornerman looks for the second cutter G
4. cornerman looks for third cutter P

Diagram 63   Diagram 64

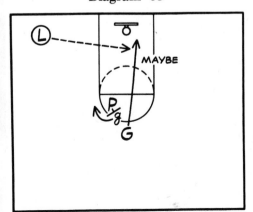

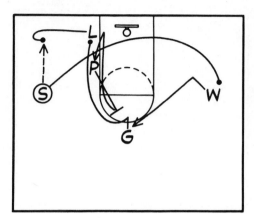

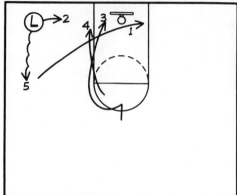

| Diagram 65 | Diagram 66 |

5. cornerman dribbles out to the wing position and a) starts 22 or b) starts another 23, Diagram 66.

Ceasing 23 and returning to weakside 22

In addition to ultimately feeding G at the middle guard position to start the weakside play (can't start or continue the weakside cycle if you can't get the ball *to* the new weakside!) we have several other effective alternatives in case we prefer not to strongside it extensively.

One way to get from 23 to 22 is to feed P at the post and let him feed either G (who will feed W, or feed W directly, Diagram 67. S may also lob the ball to W, Diagram 68.

There is an age-old rule in basketball saying this crosscourt pass is dangerous and shouldn't be done. However, we find it is not only possible, it is desirable and exerts strain on the defense

| Diagram 67 | Diagram 68 |

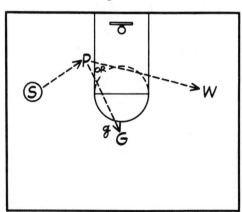

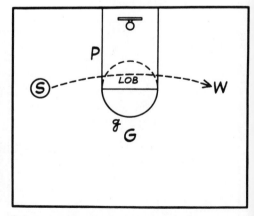

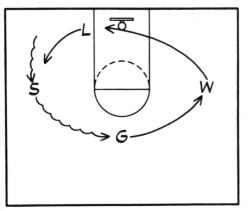

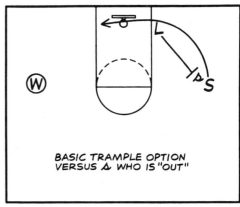

BASIC TRAMPLE OPTION
VERSUS △ WHO IS "OUT"

Diagram 69   **Diagram 70**

if done properly. The only proper way we know is with the two-hand overhead pass, which we call the lob. The pass must be from a high position to a high position and have only moderate trajectory. If it is too flat (low) defensive hands bother it, if too arched (high) it hangs too long and every defensive man in town is there waiting when it comes down.

A third way to get into 22 is for the cornerman to dribble all the way to the middle guard position and become new G as the other three perimeter men rotate away to adjacent positions, Diagram 69.

Identifying the defense

One of the first things we try to do both from the floor and from the bench is to identify the defense.

We like to know if the defense is "out," tight, meeting us early, or "in," sinking or hanging back.

VERSUS "OUT" DEFENSES

If defenses are out, we cannot push, carry or move them to an "in" position. We believe we can, however, *keep* them out. We do this of course by rear screening, by breaking by them with a lot of "vertical down" moves hoping to get to the basket as they stay "out." The Trample offense has several such techniques built in as has been demonstrated, Diagram 70. Versus the "out" defenses, we hope and expect to get a lot of board shots, lay-ups, drives, or close shots, although these shots may need to be taken somewhat quicker than leisurely!

The best we can hope for is to *keep* the defense in. We do this by screening down, i.e., front screens, and we expect to get fewer board shots and more medium distance shots. The Trample has a few such possibilities inherent.

Diagram 71 shows the G down screen on defensive p.

Diagram 72 shows again the G front screen on L who comes up to the line and *leaves* 1 "in."

Any coach who uses the Trample offense must certainly impress his players as being aggressive offensively if the defense is "out," i.e., drive, cut, go for it, etc. If not, the defense will set up business on your toes, and if the defense can, as we say "stifle" you into standing still, the game is as good as over, because the offense that is standing is a dead offense. On the other than, if the defense is "in," it will be a long night for the team who insists on forcing their way too far into the hornets' nest.

Fundamental games in the Trample offense

A complete pattern should have various ways to score including all of the free lance techniques. The Trample offense contains or can easily include the following:

GIVE-GO

As shown in Diagram 55, one give-go maneuver is a basic move in the Trample. It is also a natural for G and W to work a give-go occasionally on the weakside, Diagram 73, as G usually feeds and clears away from the ball, defensive g is usually ripe for this

Diagram 71

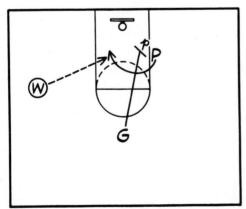

Diagram 72

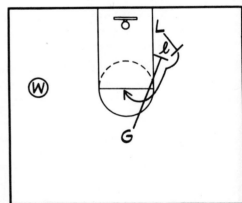

move later in the game after having been conditioned to the feed-and-clear away game.

CLEAR-OUT ON THE WEAKSIDE

Any but the poorest guards appreciate an opportunity to "show their stuff" and the clear-out maneuver affords this opportunity as well as tending to keep the defense honest. The weakside clear is quickest and easiest and is highly effective. W jockeys and at the end of his second step to the basket he makes no attempt to halt, but goes on through to the far side of the lane. The weakside of the floor is now entirely clear and G pounds leather and should be on the board in about three good bounces. He need not run a circuitous route: usually about a step outside the lane is ideal, Diagram 74. We prefer to call for this action before the ball crosses the time line, as by G inconspicuously telling W to "clear" before the Trample set is established; or we call "Clear Terry" from the bench as one of the men go by. The weakside clear can naturally be called "clear 2" as it is on the 22 or weakside.

CLEAR-OUT ON THE STRONGSIDE

It is also possible to run a good clear-out on the strongside by moving three instead of one man. On the 3 (short for 23) side, P, L, and S must leave the area, Diagram 75.

CONTINUITY IF THE CLEAR-OUT FAILS

If G is stopped before he gets the shot, he balances over to play the wing on his side and immediately starts 22, Diagram 76,

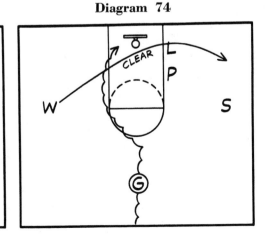

Diagram 73   **Diagram 74**

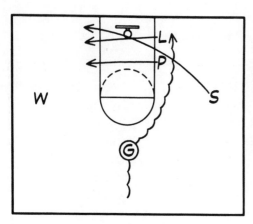

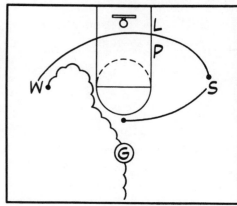

| Diagram 75 | Diagram 76 |

as W and S rotate away one position. In fact, we often start a 22 cycle with a partial clear if we have difficulty getting the feed to W; i.e., we will deliver the ball via the dribble.

The strongside clear can be blended into the Trample continuity by S going to the opposite wing as W plays G, Diagram 77. In case L and P did not clear-out along with S, Diagram 78, the man with the ball can go to the corner feed to start 23, Diagram 79.

ISOLATION

There is usually one mis-match in favor of the offense in any game. If a particular defender isn't equal to an offensive man it

| Diagram 77 | Diagram 78 |

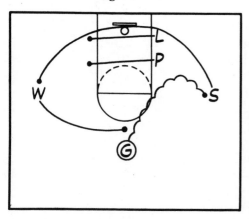

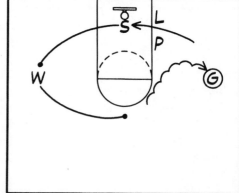

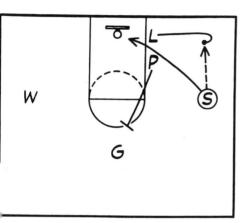
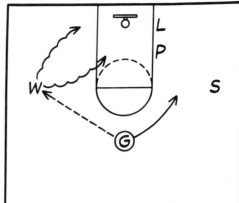

Diagram 79   **Diagram 80**

is sound basketball to put these two alone in a large floor area
and let them play one-on-one. The Trample offense has this "isolation" effect at least once every cycle. It is, of course, the first
move in 22, as G feeds W and isolates him. If we want to exploit
this fully, we tell P, L, and S to delay working to the ball, Diagram 80.

SPLITTING

As we said earlier, we try to split the post any time a man with
the ball cannot or does not attempt to score immediately if he is
near the lane (this usually means he has his back to the basket).
The two men nearest him jockey for purposes of getting their
defender at a disadvantage and then go over the post. There are
innumerable possibilities and combinations for this to occur, Diagram 81 is just an example. We don't attempt to restrict the cutters to particular players—whoever can get there first and second,
"get." If a third man gets into the act, so much tte better: the
triple split, Diagram 82.

WEAVING

Players who can dribble well plus jump shoot can be effective
with the weave. The easiest method is to operate as shown on
Diagram 83.

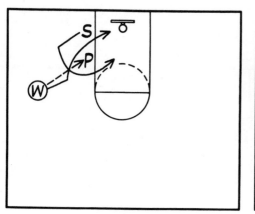

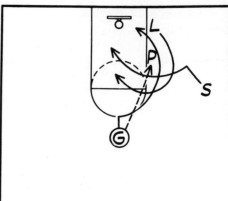

Diagram 81

Diagram 82

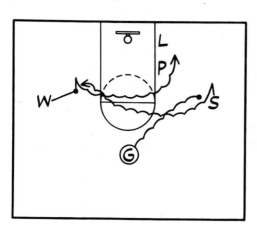

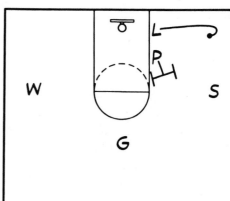

Diagram 83

Diagram 84

G moves the ball with a dribble to S who jockeys for freedom, waits for G to touch the ball with both hands—ending G's dribble —takes the ball and drives back toward the weakside, crowding in (gaining ground) as much as possible. W steps forward to preserve whatever ground was gained by S, jockeys, starts quickly when S picks up his dribble and works back to strongside where he may work over the two postmen or feed G for another cycle.

The cue or signal that we employ to start the weave is for G to *dribble* toward either wing without having signalled for the clear-out.

The four man weave is easy to use with L moving over to get into the pattern as P uses his potential as a screener, Diagram 84.

The weave game is treated more thoroughly in Chapter 4.

DOUBLE AND TRIPLE SCREENS

We have always held a high regard for double and triple screens and the Trample offense can easily make use of this offensive technique. If, for example, G would feed W and clear down the far side to a medium post position above P, a triple screen is established with W being isolated to free lance the weakside, Diagrams 85 and 86.

S can work under or over the triple screen, Diagram 87, or hang behind the screen or circle it for the lob feed from W, Diagram 88.

The further use of double and triple screens is covered in Chapter 3.

We find this to be a good bet to get a few high percentage shots

Diagram 85

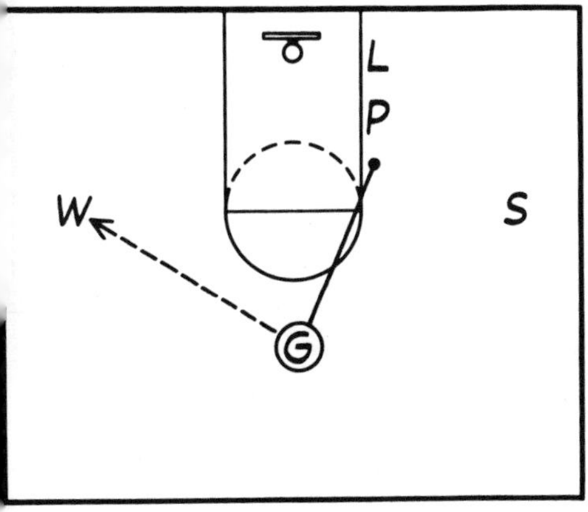

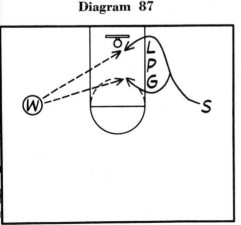

Diagram 86

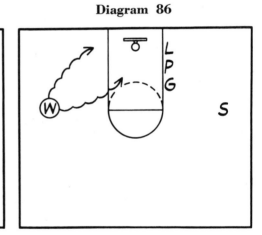

Diagram 87

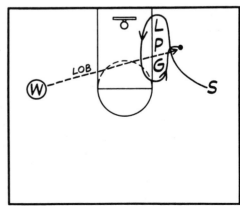

Diagram 88

perhaps near the end of a game in close contests when we are really in need of just one sure basket.

Balancing at the shot

The instant the shot leaves the shooter's hand, we change from our Trample positions to a 3 1/2 offensive balance cup. We do do this because we believe defense—if it is to begin—begins at this precise instant. We want one man immediately back to the time line, one near the top of the circle, and three men in a triangle around the board.

We usually do not assign men to a predetermined spot in the 3 1/2 cup. We do feel a priority exists and we want all men to check all five spots in priority order and fill the spot *first* if no teammate has already done so. We fill these five spots in this order, Diagram 89.

BALANCING RULES

First and most important: E, the safety spot. Get as deep as possible, if we don't get depth quickly, we're a dead duck on the fast break. *Next:* the weakside board (side opposite the side from which the shot was taken), half way between the corner of the board and the lane edge is about right. Players tend to get too close, near the edge of the rim, but few shots fall rim width. Inasmuch as the average missed shot will rebound half the distance it was shot, don't get too close! You'll probably have to prove this to your boys before they will believe it. Put a shooter out and let him miss some and see where the rebounds fall.

Third spot: front of the rim about one foot on the basket side of the dotted line interior half of the free throw circle. Don't get closer.

Fourth: near corner of the board, corresponding to the assignment of the weak corner rebound spot.

Fifth: top of key. This man is half offense and half defense. He responds to defensive commands from the safety man. He also has a two-fold offensive task: 1) he goes after all the long rebounds that fall beyond his three rebounding teammates, and 2) he expects the feed back if one of the rebound triangle men gain possession and cannot score.

Chances are any ball he gets he will be able to stick back into

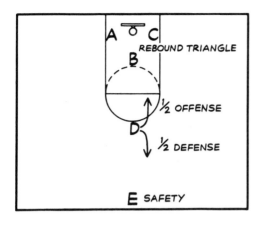

REBOUND TRIANGLE

½ OFFENSE

½ DEFENSE

Diagram 89

E SAFETY

the hoop with that very reliable 12 to 15 foot front shot. This "half" man will get a lot of points on follow-up shots.

I cannot emphasize enough the importance of balancing into the 3 1/2 cup the instant the first shot goes out of the shooter's hand.

In the daily practices, we spend considerable time running a Trample, shoot and *balancing* immediately. When balancing becomes second nature, your offense will have approached maturity and the rewards will be worth the time spent.

In summary, wherever you are, at the shot, balance 3 1/2.

Summarizing the advantages of the Trample

The Trample has served well as an offensive attack. It seems to have many requisites of a good offensive scheme and it does the following things rather well:

1. makes the defense move constantly
2. confuses the defense
3. produces the inside (short) shot or at worst, the medium distance shot
4. is fairly capable of getting the follow-up shots
5. balances easily so that the transition to defense is sound
6. is well balanced so that all defensive areas are threatened
7. enables the offensive team to control the ball thus play offense more than defense
8. threatens the defense with a variety of scoring threats, including: drives, give-go, isolation, two-on-one, weave, shuffle, splits, screen shots, etc.

41

9. adjusts quickly and without interruption to most defensive variations
10. is capable of disguise and concealment of intent by aligning in various spots only to end up in Trample position.

The Trample does all these things well. It is a pleasure to coach, a thrill to execute and a joy to see. It appears complicated to the defense and to the fans but taken step-by-step in detail— as has been done in this chapter—it is extremely simple and can be learned (but not perfected, of course) by any dedicated group of boys in one or two practice sessions.

THREE

Weakside Twin Post,

a Moderate Tempo Pattern

Rhythm is important in sports, it is important in basketball. Tempo, or rate of timing, likewise is important. Whereas the Trample is a fast, rather high rate pattern with a constant or even rhythm, the Weakside Twin Post differs by being 1) slower and 2) less rhythmic, i.e., there are spots in the continuity where action occurs fast and other options follow rapidly, and there are time intervals where one or more threats occur more deliberately. I hasten to contend that there are times when a slower and more deliberate offensive maneuver is best and therefore present this offensive scheme without any apologies when I refer to it as a "moderate tempo pattern."

We usually align in Trample formation, then move a couple of men to start the Twin Post attack.

The alignment is indicated in Diagram 90 with P about one-half step above L, as both these men face across the lane, toes nearly on the lane line and feet perpendicular to this line. C, the cornerman, is about six feet from the baseline and about twice as far from the lane as he is from his own corner. W, the wingman, is on the extended free throw line three to six feet from his side-line and G, the middle guard is on the mid line one or two steps above the key circle.

If we blend the weakside twin post game with our Trample Offense, we usually go from Trample alignment to twin post by moving the original Trample W (weakside man) down to the baseline to play C (cornerman), moving Trample G (guard) over to play the W (wing) and bringing Trample S (strongside) over to the center to play the new G (guard) position, Diagram 91.

If we do not care to first show a Trample formation, we merely come down the floor and align as in Diagram 90.

JOCKEY AND DRIVE

Either W (wing) or G (guard) may dribble the ball down the floor, although we prefer that G do so. As the ball carrier approaches his "home spot," he is always alert to a defensive lapse and if possible, will drive past his defender and try to go all the way. The other two non-post men likewise jockey for freedom as the ball carrier approaches so that they are open if and when it becomes desirable that they be fed. The center is open in this pat-

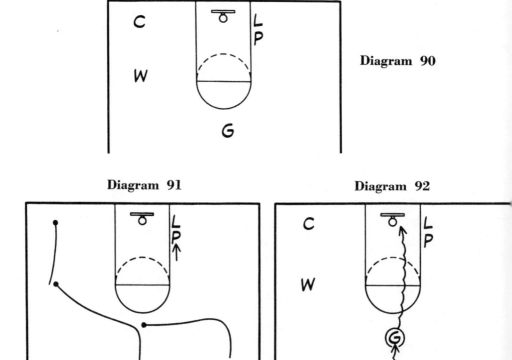

Diagram 90

Diagram 91

Diagram 92

tern and we want the drive any time we can get it, Diagram 92.
We then begin the series of options in the Weakside Twin Post.

Give-go option #1

G feeds W and starts inward. He fakes away from the ball and
then back toward the ball, then cuts down the heart of the lane
at a controlled trot. He should not hurry; hurrying will enhance
his give-go potential but will result in too-frequent charge fouls.
As he goes down the lane he is alert for a return feed from W,
usually late—just as he goes under the rim, Diagram 93. We seldom get this first option and not infrequently the return pass
bounces off his ear and into the bleachers as he has been surprised
at his own game!

If G receives no return on the give-go he fades away from the
ball-side and goes behind the Twin Posts and usually on the baseline side of L who is one step higher than the board or about
seven feet from the baseline, Diagram 94.

Give-go option #2

Immediately upon receiving the initial feed from G, W consid-
ers driving on his defender and will do so if w is out of position.
This drive must occur *immediately* if it is to occur; we do not
permit any deliberation on the part of W. If, after checking out
defensive w there is no *defensive* weakness, the wingman W instantly looks to the corner and unless defensive c is in interception
position, W *immediately* feeds C and goes at the basket *fast*. C
returns the ball on the give-go, if possible. This is Option #2 and
it occurs much more frequently for us than does the first option,
Diagram 95.

Diagram 93   Diagram 94

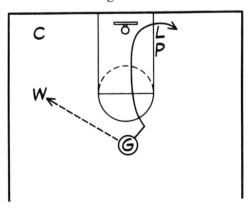

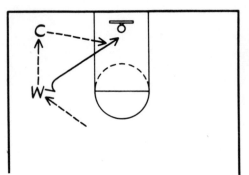

Diagram 95

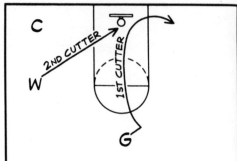

Diagram 96

These two options occur "zip ... zip" about one and one-half seconds apart if done properly. As soon as G has cleared the lane and started around the twin posts, W is coming fast. We refer to these two men as the first cutter (G) and the second cutter (W), Diagram 96.

The second cutter, W, goes through the lane and begins to work around the twin posts. C has now been isolated and has his half of the floor to himself and his defender. The third option is now ready to begin.

Isolation

C can occasionally feed the first cutter G if W gets the feed to C quickly, Diagram 97. This is a better give-go than the W to G maneuver mentioned previously as Option #1.

If C does not feed G or W, he tries to work his defender by driving baseline side or top-side of his defender *if* his defender is *tight*, Diagram 98. If defensive c is loose, C can pop in the 15 to 17 foot set or jumper, Diagram 99. This is Option #3.

Diagram 97   **Diagram 98**

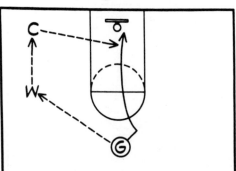

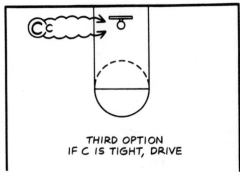

THIRD OPTION
IF C IS TIGHT, DRIVE

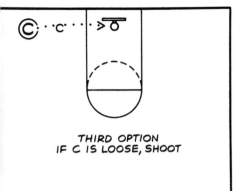

THIRD OPTION
IF C IS LOOSE, SHOOT

Diagram 99

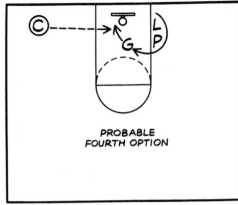

PROBABLE
FOURTH OPTION

Diagram 100

Post cutters

As C is working for the drive or shot, the first and second cutters are attempting to free themselves from defensive men by rubbing them off on the double screen effect of the twin posts. The most common maneuver is the first cutter coming around L and P and moving ball-side again for the ball-side lay up on a feed from C, Diagram 100. This is normally our fourth option and is usually one of the better options. Defensive g is apt to be caught behind the double screen if he pursues G around (to the far side) the twin posts.

In executing this cut around the posts, G must come close to P, fast, and lean into the curve as he bows into the ball-side corner of the board. The feed should be about forehead high and brisk. As the cutter takes this lay-up he should crowd into the board and face the baseline. He must go into the board and rim with his entire weight and not fade away.

Reversing

After G has circled the posts for the lay-up, defensive men may begin to "play-the-play" and wait for G at the top of the twin posts, Diagram 101; or go through (between L and P), Diagram 102; or go directly behind the twin posts to arrive there before G and thus be better prepared to avert the rub-off on the return cut, Diagram 103.

If any of these three defensive tricks are employed, G "re-

47

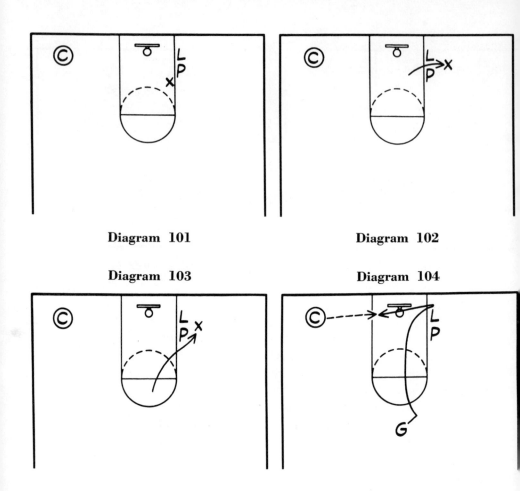

Diagram 101   Diagram 102

Diagram 103   Diagram 104

verses" and comes back to the ball in lieu of circling the posts, Diagram 104. This reverse maneuver may become the fourth option, as the circle of the posts (which might follow an unsuccessful reverse) would become Option #5.

Lobbing

If defensive g refuses to go behind the double screen, if he will not chase G away from the ball, or if he is rubbed off on the front side of the posts as G leaves the lane, G may go behind the posts about 2 steps beyond the posts and stand. G signals with a raised arm, C uses the 2 hand overhead lob to feed G. G then has the eight to ten foot screen shot, Diagram 105. As this maneuver is usually set-up by success in the fourth option, we usually refer to it as Option #5, although it may actually be the sixth scoring threat.

48

In discussing these latter three options we have not mentioned W, the second cutter. Actually W does exactly the same things as does G; we have limited the examples to one man for the sake of clarity. There are two men working in and about the twin posts and the possibilities of this combination of two men and three options (#4, #5, and #6) are about a dozen in number. A few examples are now in order.

G may circle for the lay-up, followed by W doing likewise two or three steps later, Diagram 106.

G and W may repeat this fairly simple stunt a second time, Diagram 107.

G may circle as W waits behind and signals for the lob, Diagram 108, or G may play lob as W circles. We do not permit two men to hang back and simultaneously ask for the lob.

One cutter may go behind and then reverse "late"; we call this the "come-under," Diagram 109, as the other cutter plays lob, or plays follow the leader and reverses late, or cuts over the posts.

These are simple maneuvers but they must be practiced in drill to be reliable and effective under pressure. This makes for a good shooting and ball handling session. The weakside twin post is a good offense partly because of the ease with which parts of it can be extracted for drill work. Put two managers in the post position and a feeder at C; then send cutters around, back under, reversing, standing for the lob, etc.

As these latter three options are developing, C is either waiting (but not long) or working for a shot. If defensive c does not

Diagram 105	Diagram 106

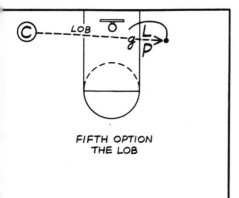

FIFTH OPTION
THE LOB

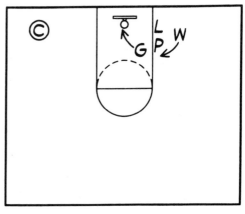

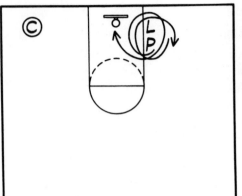

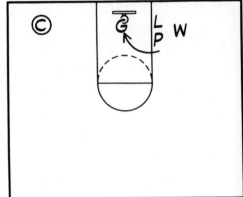

Diagram 107   Diagram 108

molest C, it is fine for C to wait the two to six seconds as the cutters act. If C is liable to the five-second count, he may crowd in
toward the lane with a bounce, or two or three, then feed a cutter
or make a lob. The dribbling of C may be slow or apparently
wasteful, but the bouncing of the ball often detracts defensive
attention from the action going on about the twin posts, Diagram 110.

Breaking out

The two post men, L (low post) and P (post or high post)
are instructed *not* to invite themselves to the ball-side of the floor
unless they are unmistakably unmolested and free for an easy
shot. We do not want them to clutter up the isolated side of the
floor since we want it kept open for feeding of cutters and for C

Diagram 109   Diagram 110

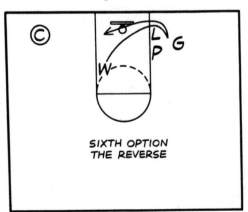

SIXTH OPTION
THE REVERSE

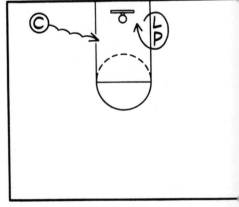

to free lance. We also, obviously, will not have a double screen if
L or P come across the lane.

If, however, P or L is not defended on the ballside, they may
"break-out" of the twin post position to a spot from which they
may receive the feed from C and shoot or drive, Diagram 111.
The break-out occurs as a result of defensive post men 1 and p
switching to pick up cutters or lob men and their defensive assignments not being assumed by teammates. The break-out is Option
#7.

Dragging across the lane

If nothing develops in the first seven options, we now expect
C to do his best to bring the ball across the lane. This "drag" can
be a shuffling type dribble with C's back toward the basket. C
must make his defensive man baseline conscious at all times,
which makes it considerably easier to "drag" over the top.

If C has a hook shot, he can score a lot of points as he approaches mid lane—he can usually work to a distance of eight to
ten feet, Diagram 112. This is Option #8.

Driving over the twin post

If C is not a hook shooter or if this shot is undesirable, C can
often drag across the lane and attempt to rub defensive c off on
P, then shoot over the double screen with the eight foot jumper,
Diagram 113, Option #9, or bow down to the baseline for the
board shot, Diagram 114.

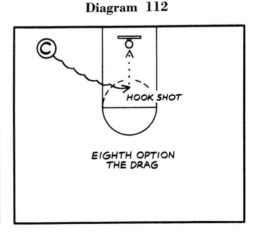

Diagram 111

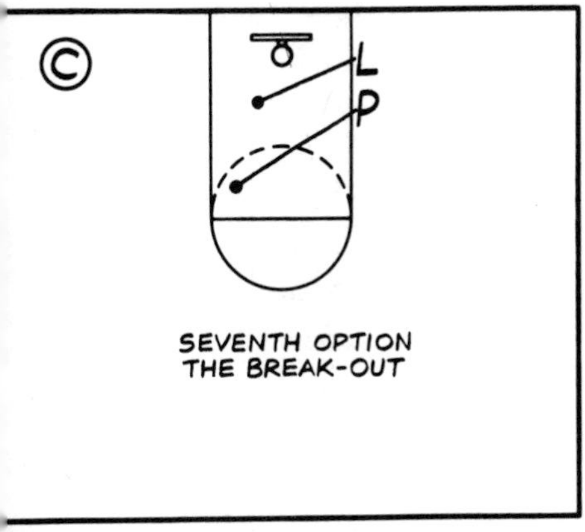

Diagram 112

SEVENTH OPTION
THE BREAK-OUT

EIGHTH OPTION
THE DRAG

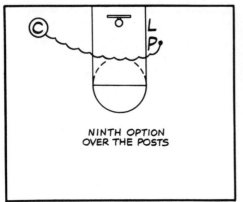

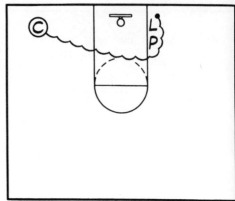

Diagram 113   Diagram 114

Stepping out and rolling over

If C has no shot opening after having gone over the double
screen, as in diagrams 113 or 114, he may pull in his dribble and
pivot away from the basket as the high post P steps behind him
quickly, accepts the ball and tries for a shot using the feeder C
as a screen, Diagram 115. If P is not able to try this, or if he tries
and cannot accept the feed, he goes on by to the baseline near
the lane, Diagram 116, and as soon as he clears the area we expect
L to do the same thing from his low post position, i.e., roll over
C, Diagram 117. To complete this tenth option, the two cutters
W and G have returned to a floor balance position. Probably one
is at the top of the key and the other ready to rebound the weakside of the board, Diagram 118.

Diagram 115   Diagram 116

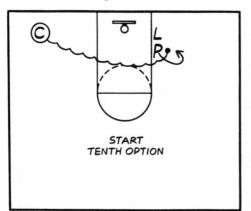

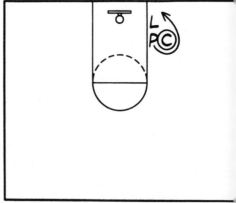

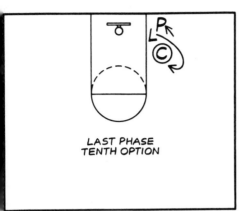

LAST PHASE
TENTH OPTION

Diagram 117

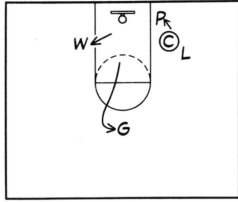

Diagram 118

Splitting

There have been three opportunities for post men to shoot in these last three options, #8, #9, and #10. The stepping out and rolling over of the twin posts is a type of splitting. We maintain our previously stated post-split rule however, and "Anytime a man has the ball near the basket or lane and does not or cannot score immediately, the two nearest teammates must split him." These two nearest men may be L and P, as we indicated above, or they may be G and W coming from the outside, Diagram 119. This split opportunity or option #11, may occur any time, at any spot on the floor with any man, as the post man, with any two men splitting, and may evolve as any option other than the eleventh.

Continuing (continuity)

A shot will usually ensue before the eleven options are expended. We like to maintain a long-range continuity outlook and plan to operate another full series in case we do not get the shot we like.

In maintaining the attitude that we will repeat the series again or perhaps several times, we now consider our plan to begin again. This we do by merely sending G, W and C back home and begin again, Diagram 120.

We may change sides and go opposite, with each man reversing or mirroring his floor position, Diagram 121.

If L and P are versatile, we interchange positions and let them

53

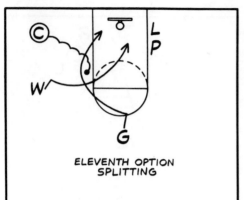

ELEVENTH OPTION
SPLITTING

Diagram 119

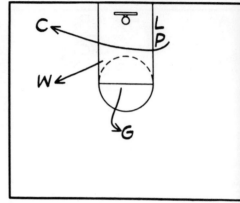

Diagram 120

play a wing or a corner position, Diagram 122. We consider it a good idea to have our four largest men play, in practice, all four positions (C, W, P, and L). We also drill our three smaller men (W, G, and another) to play each of these three front positions.

WEAKNESSES

The one problem is that there are times when both front men (W and G) are "in" and, as a result, there is no defensive balance. If we lose the ball at this time there is a scramble for the far end and we are at a disadvantage.

Balancing for rebounding

Although we are at times without a safety man back, we are confident of getting a good shot and do not worry about that factor.

Diagram 121

Diagram 122

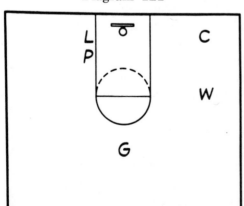

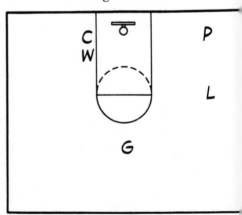

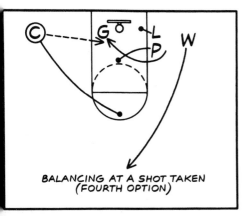

BALANCING AT A SHOT TAKEN
(FOURTH OPTION)

Diagram 123

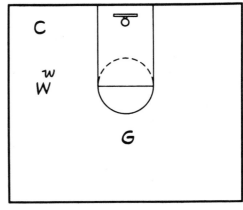

Diagram 124

The rebounding is sound since the adjustments to a 3 1/2 cup is effected. The deepest man should scramble to mid-court at the shot, the three men nearest the board should set the rebound triangle, and the last man should go for the "1/2" spot. Should a shot occur, for example, on the fourth option with G circling for the lay-up, W would get back, C to the top of the key, P to the center of the triangle and L rebound weakside corner, Diagram 123.

Variations versus defensive adjustments

The most common defensive adjustments are as follows: 1) If defensive wingmen attempt to keep us from getting the ball to the corner, Diagram 124, we encourage the drive by W to the key with G going early to clear the lane, Diagram 125. G can also feed W and screen inside on w to allow the drive to the key by

Diagram 125

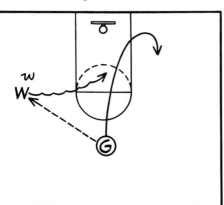

Diagram 126

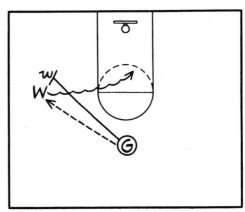

W, Diagram 126. This can include, in addition, a rear screen by C or W, although usually this is an unnecessary move. 2) If defensive c overplays C effectively, C can clear as W drives baseline on the W clear-out play, Diagram 127, or feed C as he clears. 3) If defensive g sags excessively or jams up the post circling of G and/or W, G can fade away or stay out rather than go in on his cut, Diagram 128. As the other options are developing, G can then use discretion and work into the picture from the far side and make use of rear screens to rub off defensive g, Diagram 129, or he may start in front of the posts and fade again for the lob, Diagram 130. 4) Occasionally it is helpful to use the first cutter as a third post man, then use C as a feeder as W works his

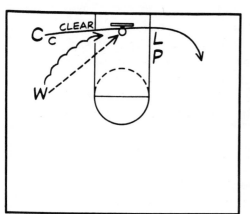

Diagram 127

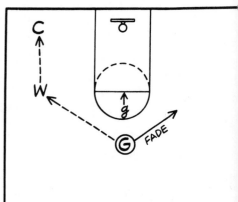

Diagram 128

Diagram 129

Diagram 130

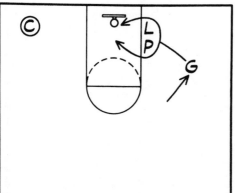

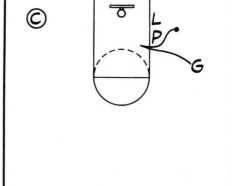

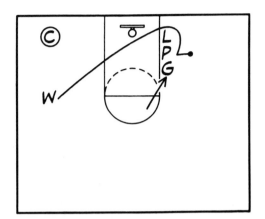

Diagram 131

options around a triple weakside post, Diagram 131. 5) The other major defensive adjustment is zone defense. Chapter 6 explains how this pattern adjusts to zones. This is incidentally our favorite zone attack pattern.

FOUR

Dribbling Continuity, an Auxiliary Trample

Whereas the Trample is basically a passing game as is the Weakside Twin Post, there certainly is something to be said in favor of a dribbling offense. If the alignment can be arranged so that extensive dribbling is possible, then a dribbling game is a *safe* game, but promiscuous dribbling often results in being double-teamed, loose balls, etc. If a coach has two or more good dribblers who can jump shoot, this offense might be useful. We've had a million thrills with it over several seasons at three levels of competition, junior high, senior high, and college. It is similar to our Trample, except for the work of one man.

Simplicity and other advantages

From Trample formation, Diagram 132, we move W to the strongside corner and raise P to the line, Diagram 133. This opens the left side for ensuing action. Should a team have two or more left-handers, it is best to overload the right side; should this not be the case, then it is best to change over to the left.

We prefer to Trample once (on cycle), starting strong right,

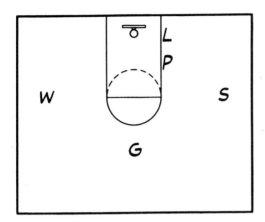

Diagram 132

Diagram 133

Diagram 134

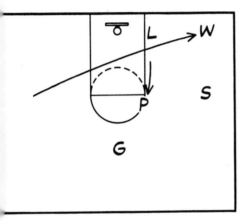

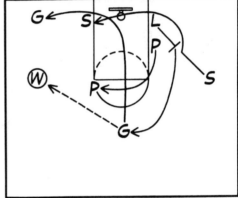

then overload left by sending G to the *ball-side* corner instead of away from the ball, Diagram 134.

Lay-up potential

In general, we try to: 1) weave the three outside men over the high post and under the low post for lay-ups, usually working from the overload side to the open side; 2) work an abrupt weave game for jump shots over the posts; 3) use a couple of good, simple but more deliberate plays.

The weave best begins with the ball at W, the middle man of the three. W can begin by going either right (to G) or left (to the corner).

One weave maneuver which is likely to get a free man quickly to the wide open spaces on the right side is shown in Diagram 135, as W feeds G and clears away to screen C. C comes up to meet G coming strongside, accepts the ball and tries to drive over the new high post L (who has meanwhile interchanged with P, which keeps defensive p from switching on the driver C). C has a good chance of rubbing his man, c, off on L who is looking (hunting) for c, Diagram 136.

If l switches on C, L can run down the lane for the "dummy" play feed from C before defensive c can get position on L to complete the switch, Diagram 137. We always tell our high post man to break down their own side of the lane to the basket any time

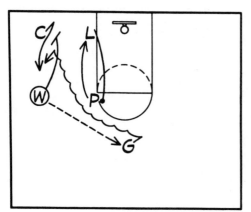

Diagram 135

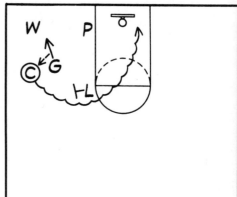

Diagram 136

Diagram 137

Diagram 138

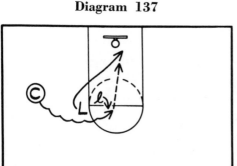

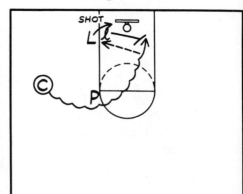

there is a teammate driving down the other side of the lane. This gives the driver a lay-back outlet if he encounters a switch.

The usual result on any free driver going down the open (right) side is for the defensive low post man to switch over and take him. The driver then feeds short across the lane and the low post has a left side lay-up, Diagram 138.

The weave also works well if started first to the corner by W dribbling to C, C dribbling up to meet G, G bouncing to W who is recovering from the corner. W then has G's screen to work over, plus the high post. The post men may interchange or stay in original positions, Diagram 139.

Whereas the weave shown in Diagram 135 (which isn't a true weave, but a pass and screen-away maneuver) is short and (usually) sweet, the more complete weave with the three exchanges shown in Diagram 139 has more threats, such as the following: 1) C may break back the "wrong" way if defensive c expects him to go up and out, Diagram 140. 2) C may break *through* the gap and go under P rather than over him, or go to meet G, Diagram 141. 3) W may pass C, keep the ball and drive to the baseline as L steps up for a rear screen on w, Diagram 142. This is a fine two-man play. If L gets a good screen, defensive 1 must let W go to the board or switch. If 1 switches, W gives L the lay-over on the roll (commonly called the pick and roll), Diagram 143. 4) G can ignore W coming up and go for the drive at various points: (a) wrong way over P, (b) through the gap, or (c) pick and roll at L, Diagram 144. 5) Any weave dribbler may shoot over either post. The easiest shot to get is the jumper over P following a weave, Diagram 145.

Diagram 139

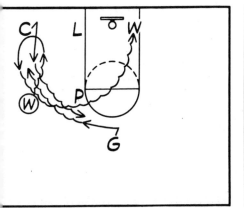

Diagram 140

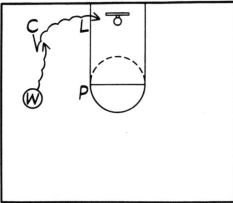

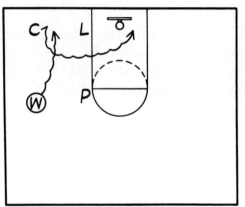

Diagram 141

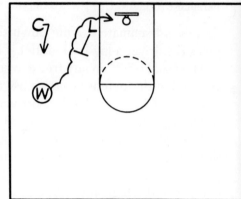

Diagram 142

Diagram 143

Diagram 144

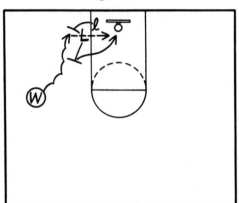

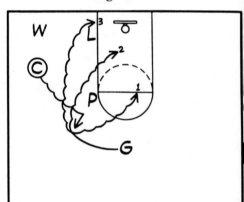

Medium distance jump shots over screens

In addition to the jump shot over a post man, jump shots are the best complement to the drive-for-the-lay-up. The usual defensive adjustment to stop the lay-up drive from the weave is to loosen up, go behind screens, switch on all crosses, or zone it. The jump shot from outside then falls appropriately into place.

A simple way to get the jumper is to feed P and split him, then two near men go by for the feed out by P and the shot, Diagram 146. We like to encourage the two splitters to run over and past P and if they are not fed, to abruptly stop and come back over him

62

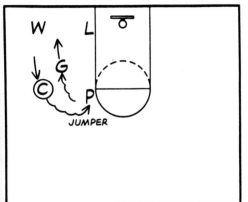

Diagram 145

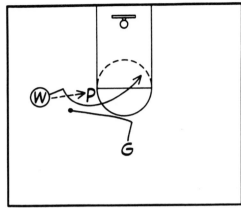

Diagram 146

again (and again) in an oscillation split until finally a defensive man is squeezed into the jam. Diagram 147 shows W doing just this; naturally G would also be involved.

WEAKNESSES

We've never relied solely on this one offense for an entire season, although perhaps it is sound enough. If a coach has strong outside shooters it should be sound. If not, we doubt that it could beat the switching defenses and the zone.

It likewise is not the best if L is a weak rebounder.

Basic pattern movement

A very effective play was accidentally conceived on one occasion as we asked G to clear-out down the lane so C could "bring it around." The clear-out I was seeking is shown in Diagram 148. This is a good maneuver after having operated the weave. The

Diagram 147

Diagram 148

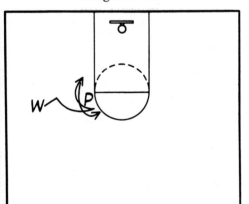

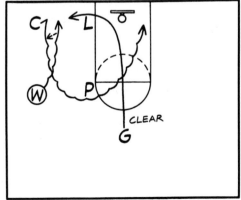

W man saw G coming back into the corner and became confused. W went under the board to a spot on the opposite lane base, Diagram 149. C came around, was stopped at the line, so he stopped and fed W. G, in the meantime, had cleared down, came back up the strongside for balance, saw W receive the feed and immediately peeled around L (who was interchanging with P), back down to the basket for a lay-up feed from W, Diagram 150.

Since that "boo-boo" several years ago we've pulled this one hundreds of times. In brief:

W: weaves to the corner, feeds off and clears to the open side lane base and faces in

G: clears out when W starts his dribble and then circles in again

L and P: interchange

C: accept weave hand-off from W, crowd around and drive it down for the shot, or feed W who shoots or feeds G, Diagram 151.

Variations versus Defensive Adjustments

If the defense plays tight the weave is best, or the post feed and split.

If the defense switches, go to the jump shorts or to the "wrong way" reverse dribbles.

If the post men are played man-to-man, L and P should interchange. There are two ways to operate this interchange.

If the defense is tight or high on L and P, the interchange should occur from the inside *out* (or from low to high, i.e., screen *out*, Diagram 152. This follows the principle of "keep the defense out if it is out."

If the defense is "in" or sinking, Diagram 153, it is best to screen "down," i.e., P moving first to front screen l, Diagram 154. Probably defensive p is so loose from P that he would escape or recover from any rear screen set on him by L.

If one post man is not a strong rebounder or scorer, he can be of good use at the high post P serving as a screener. L should be the better of the two men. One good outside man can dribble the ball down and move around until he gets on the back of one of his buddies for a screen jumper, or until he finds a chance to get

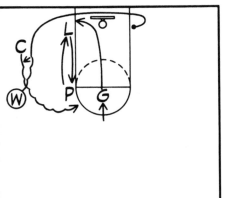

Diagram 149

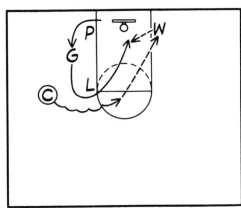

Diagram 150

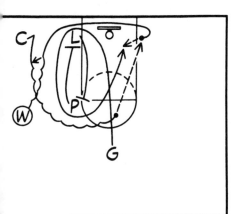

Diagram 151

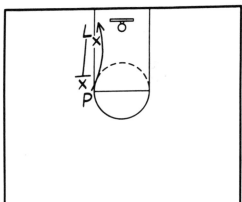

Diagram 152

Diagram 153

Diagram 154

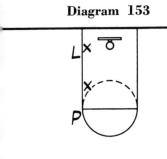

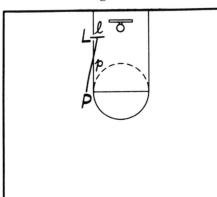

to the wide open right side. This isolation potential on the right side is all that is needed if the one man is good enough. This can then be a good one-man pattern.

One cold January night a little corner man of mine came around the high post and down the open side for easy lay-ups 14 times in the first quarter—against the county champions, no less! Obviously it was too easy—he blew 13! No pattern is effective without fundamental skills.

FIVE

Twin Tandem Posts;

Deliberate Game

In one recent season we were able to maintain a successful offensive attack with the Trample. There were certain critical occasions during the season when I developed grave doubts about our chances of winning unless we could do something unusual or unique. In the latter stages of these (six) close and tough contests, we went to what we call the "ABS" game, and won five going away. This game is one I consider to be a "one-man" game, with twin posts on each side of the lane.

This concept is not original with us. We have seen or heard about its use on several occasions. It is unique, however, to our situation because of 1) the uses to which we put it, or the situations in which we use it (purposes), 2) the techniques we employ (how) we use it, 3) the fact that we *do* use it and that we have not encountered it otherwise in our area.

Most important, it is: 1) easily learned, 2) does not detract from the regular offense, 3) is fun for the players, 4) exploits special abilities of certain players, 5) tends to produce points in critical contests by producing close shots.

Use as a semi-freeze attack

A main purpose for which ABS can be employed is as a semi-freeze when we want and need perhaps only one basket, yet need to control the ball and not hurry. ABS can give the "keep-away" effect as we go for a sure one.

The best ball handler and shooter should occupy the A position, Diagram 155. This is the prime or "A-1" spot. This boy must be able to dribble, have an outside shot and a confidence in his ability to maintain control of the ball versus one aggressive defender. He likewise must be aggressive, yet he cannot afford to be impetuous; he must have patience and not be too score hungry lest he hurry and take the bad shot.

The two *big* men (B for big), assume medium posts facing across the lane with feet perpendicular to the lane sides. They must exercise patience and not move from this position except on limited occasions.

The smaller two remaining men align at high posts and face the top of the key circle, since they need to see the side court area in the vicinity of the extended free throw line.

In the semi-freeze situations we expect A to score 1) a lay-up, 2) a 15 foot jumper, or 3) be fouled, preferably as he is shooting —not as he plays freeze—we want a three point play.

A tries first and foremost to get the ball down to the board by going first down the lane center directly after a good fake on

Diagram 155

Diagram 156

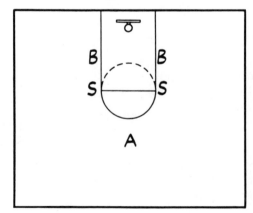
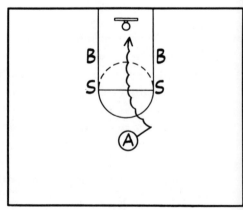

defensive a, Diagram 156, or by first starting to a side and then rubbing a on the outside or front of the screen by S, Diagram 157. This is the primary maneuver. Although I don't expect to get it frequently or consistently, we feel we must make the opponents respect it. If either defensive s man switches in the lane, Diagram 158, A will lay-back to S who has the 13 foot jumper, Diagram 159.

After having established our primary intent to ram the ball down the lane center for the board lay-up and laying-back to any one of the four post men should a defensive lane man jump switch, we are now able to better exploit the outside drive to the corner of the board, Diagram 160. A should jab step toward defensive a and attempt to drive him back 1/2 step. If this step is made as a

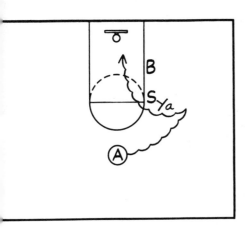

Diagram 157

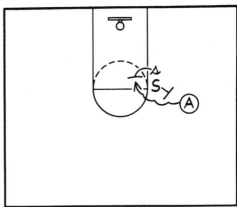

Diagram 158

Diagram 159

Diagram 160

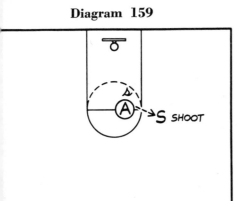

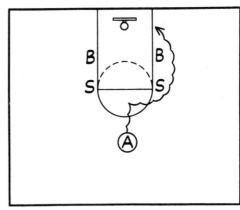

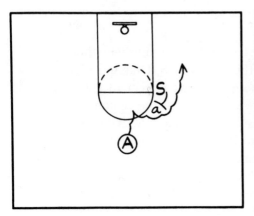
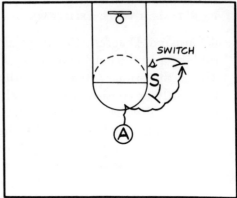

| Diagram 161 | Diagram 162 |

pivot step without a dribble, A can then go right or left. A skims very close to S who stands tough expecting defensive a to crack him. B does likewise and A tries to get to the board corner and stretch up for the side lay-up.

If A cannot crowd closely to S as he peels around the post, S should step out one step and try to catch defensive a on the screen, Diagram 161. If defensive s jump switches, Diagram 162, A should look to the lane for S going on the roll play, Diagram 163.

This inside jam and outside peel are enhanced if A will go left as often as right, thus preventing overplay by any defensive man.

There are then only two basic moves for A. He will cram down the throat of the lane very aggressively or he will peel to the outside, each time having first faked otherwise.

In this fashion the semi-freeze is usually accomplished with seldom a need to pass the ball even once, which contributes to fewer errors.

A favorite sequence to the lane jam—outside peel moves—is the clear-out. It can be done with B clearing as S stands or steps out to screen, Diagram 164, or with both B and S clearing, Diagram 165, or with B clearing as S sneaks vertically forward to screen defensive a early, Diagram 166.

Use as a high percentage short shot offense

The other four men become involved as potential scorers in a few select ways. Because the total defense tends to react and face to the ball, the following little maneuver tends to free a B (big

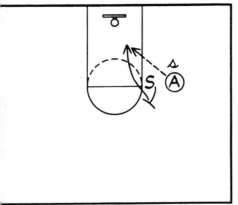

Diagram 163

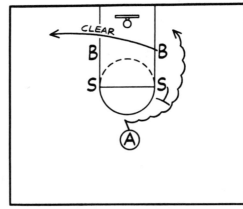

Diagram 164

Diagram 165

Diagram 166

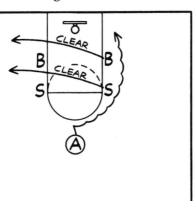

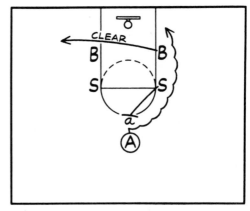

man) for a close jumper. A fakes the jam and as defensive b, s, and a tend to go to the lane, it is relatively easy to get the ball down to B with an outside feed, Diagram 167. B can then work for a board shot or a quick jumper. This works equally well right or left. We refer to this as the "reverse step-out."

The "clear and feed" is a natural sequence to the reverse step out. A and B first fake a reverse step out, then A bounces a time or two before feeding B as he comes outside under the double screens of the opposite side tandem post, Diagram 168.

Basic movements and strategies

Initially we tell the team that this is almost a one-man game. A

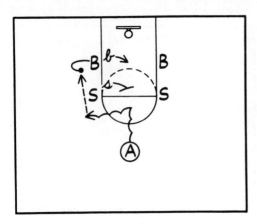

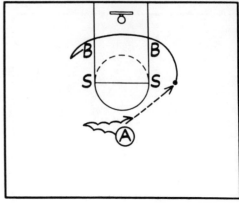

Diagram 167   Diagram 168

is the one man, the other four are more or less "out of it" until
A invites them to help. A common error is for B or S men to invite
themselves into the play. This usually disrupts the plans of A who
has all he can do in avoiding defensive a and executing his attack
plan.

General guides for B and S men are: 1) stay in place and do
not get into A's possible traffic route, 2) balance (rebound or get
back) at the shot or loss of ball, 3) wait your turn; perhaps next
time down the floor you can play the A position. 4) When you step
out to pick for A do so early enough that you are legal, 5) if the
pick is effective, hold it as long as it is effective, then roll to the
basket expecting the feed, 6) and last: you must invite yourself
to the aid of A if he gets into trouble and needs to unload the
ball. A is in trouble any time he must pull up his dribble and cannot. Because of defensive pressure, shoot or feed more or less
immediately.

Variations versus defensive adjustments

Two unit or team techniques are employed as more deliberate
scoring patterns. The first of these is the weave, which is employed
if the defense tends to run with us in a sink (loose) manner. A
crowds either right or left and tries to round the S post man. Only
when A touches the ball with both hands is the weave "on." The
nearest man (B or S) *then* steps out, goes behind A and takes the
ball, Diagram 169 and Diagram 170.

The recipient then begins normal weave technique, working
back to the far side, Diagram 171, and as he does so, being alert

72

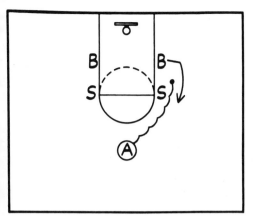

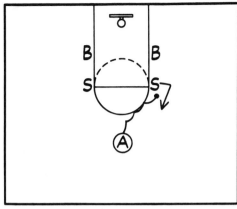

Diagram 169   **Diagram 170**

to any possibility such as reversing back to the baseline, jamming down the lane, shooting over a teammate, rounding the other side, or handing off to continue the weave, Diagram 172.

The ABS game is an excellent weave formation, the person who unloaded the weave dribble merely steps into a vacated tandem post spot, stays there until the weave dribbler touches the ball with both hands (a sign the dribble is ended). We insist that expected recipients of the weave hand-off *stand* until the dribble ends. Then they go *fast* and *quickly*.

The second five-man pattern we employ is what might be called a "special play." We have only one of these each season in case we need one basket as time is expiring. It is designed to get us a close shot near the baseline. It demands some well-timed drill to be perfected. It is a little screen play involving a feed, a step-out, and a rear split over a screen in the lane, Diagram 173. As B

Diagram 171   **Diagram 172**

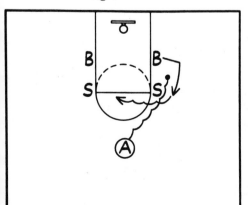

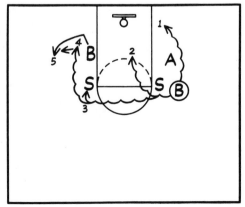

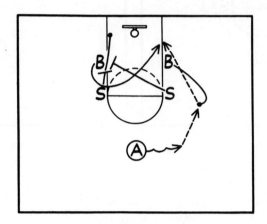

Diagram 173

waits for the clear-out screen by S and the rear split which follows, he may free lance for a shot. Otherwise, he tries to hit the
opposite B who is working around the double screen effect of both
S men. The first splitter (left S) acts as a first screener for left B,
then goes on down to his corner of the board to rebound the shot
which either B should get from the right side. The cue for this
"Blue Plate Special" can be a word by A, such as "go," or "Blue,"
etc. A makes a move to the right to start it that way, or vice versa.

SIX

Zone Attacks

Identifying zones

Before one can solve the problem of zone defenses, one must: 1) be sure that it *is* actually a zone and 2) see the true nature of it, if it is a zone.

There are several tests of a defense which are popularly employed to prove whether it is zone or man-to-man. Among these are: running a cutter from the front through to the baseline, crossing a forward through from one side to the other, dispersing and checking the number of defensive men who give primary attention to the ball, running two cutters through the defense at about the same time and route, etc. All of these ideas are good; no single one is an adequate test against the better zones which make adjustments to certain offensive movements. We attempt first of all to run our basic man-to-man pattern, which has several of these zone test movements included inherently. After our continuity has evolved through several cycles, we can conclude what the "effect" of the defense is on *us*. We do not want to be misled by: 1) teams that appear to be playing zone, but aren't, 2) teams that actually and sincerely attempt to play zone but get man-to-man effect in spite of their efforts, 3) teams that appear to be playing man-to-man, but aren't, 4) teams that actually and sin-

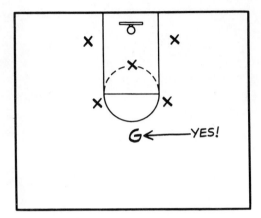

Diagram 174

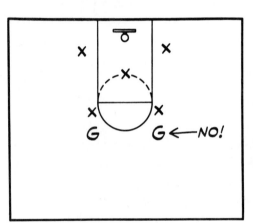

Diagram 175

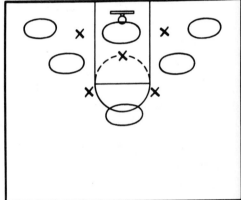

Diagram 176

cerely attempt to play man-to-man but get zone effect in spite of their efforts.

In all cases, our first contention is that we should operate our man-to-man offense and evaluate our effect. If we can make our Trample, for example, work, we care very little whether the defense is a zone or not. If our man-to-man attack will not produce, we consider it zone in spite of the theories or appearance of the opponents.

Summary of zone attack principles

All of the various zone attack patterns we may employ are governed by a few simple rules: 1) don't knot up; maintain dispersion (otherwise one defender can cover two or more); 2) hunt for the holes (every zone has holes; plan to operate from these holes or move into them appropriately); 3) be patient (don't be hurried into only outside shooting); 4) move (don't let the defense, because it is a zone, stifle you into standing still. This gives them man-to-man coverage without their earning it and without exertion on their part); 5) don't dribble much, but you can and must drive at certain times; 6) you can screen defenders (no law against this, there is no zone immunity against screens); 7) look for your teammates, move the ball, and work it inside—it can be done.

Of these general rules, we believe the second is most important. In fact, rule 2 tends to govern the attack pattern employed versus the zone.

Attacking "flathead" (two-man front) zones

If a defense is a two-guard defense such as a 2-1-2, 2-3 we will use a middle guard, Diagram 174. We may or may not use a wing-man on both sides, but we will refuse to align in a two-guard offense because we are then accommodating the defense by standing where they are strongest and accepting man-to-man coverage (the best kind, incidentally) from them. A second very important reason is that we do not want to expend any more men than necessary this far from our basket. I very much dislike playing basketball out on the front line. I want that ball to go to the baseline immediately and I want to have as many men as possible there with it. If one guard can handle it, it is a waste to use two, but primarily, the one guard can align in the natural hole (the center) of the flat zone whereas two guards cannot, Diagram 175.

Because the natural holes of 2-1-2 and 2-3 zones are similar, Diagram 176, they can be attacked with the following patterns.

High Post and Baserunner Offense

Probably the most popular zone is the 2-1-2 and, likewise, the most popular zone attack is the 1-3-1 alignment, Diagram 177. Whether the latter is true because it is appropriate versus a 2-1-2, or because of its popularity, without an understanding of why, is a moot point. There are no doubt countless coaches who consider

the old popular 1-3-1 attack as the cure for all zones, since indeed
some teams use it as their only zone weapon.

We call the 1-3-1 offense "Able." We usually name offenses
which are designed to operate against man-to-man defenses with
a number, e.g., 21, 22, and offenses designed for attacking zones
with letters from the front of the alphabet. "Able" is the universal
code word for A, which is our most-used, or first or "A-1" zone
attack. We have the following operational guides for Able, in
addition to the General Principles applying to all zones which
we mentioned earlier. See Diagram 178.

Guard

1. Don't drive the ball into the defense unless you can shoot
   from within the circle or feed off.
2. Zip the ball into the baserunner, B, any time you can.
3. Stay on the center line and don't move sideward too often
   or too much.
4. If you do move sideward, move your entire body; do not
   try to "reach around" a guard to feed a forward.
5. If a guard pressures you, it is usually best to feed the forward on the side from which pressure came.

Forwards

1. Remain alert to your primary traffic lane, Diagram 179, and
   use it any time it isn't properly defended.
2. You may go anywhere and should help the other players,
   but the other players do not help you. This freedom for F

Diagram 177   **Diagram 178**

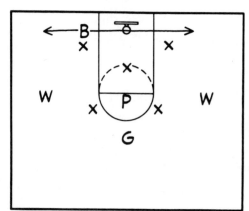   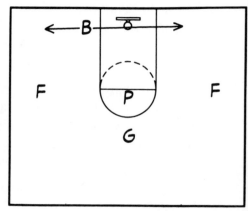

helps us to keep 6 or 7 spots filled with five men, Diagram
180.

3. If your G gets into trouble bail him out quickly.
4. Do not bury yourself behind any defender.

Baserunner

1. Spend as much time as possible under the board and at low
   post, and don't let yourself be buried behind any defender.
2. You may go to the deep corners only as a last resort.
3. Give considerable attention to P, his location and his possibilities.
4. F's will look for you.

Post Man

1. Make yourself available by moving to holes, showing us your
   location (hands, etc.).
2. Face in immediately upon receipt of ball if possible and be
   alert to your man, B.
3. P and B may alternate somewhat at the low and medium
   post and along the middle baseline.

We consider Able to be a good zone attack, but too popular.
It is one of the standard or widely-used offenses. Because of the
tremendous advantages of being different, we prefer to use some
other less popular standard defense or some variation of our regular man-to-man patterns. We have a Trample Zone attack and a
Weakside Twin Post Zone attack which we will discuss later.

Diagram 179   **Diagram 180**

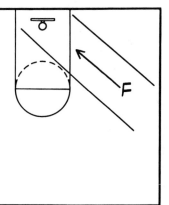

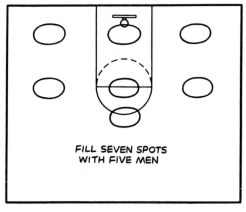

FILL SEVEN SPOTS
WITH FIVE MEN

CORNER OVERLOAD OFFENSE

If you have a good corner shooter, the following pattern can exert pressure on a flathead zone. I consider, incidentally, the deep corner as the most difficult of all spots from which to score. The shooter sees only a 5/8″ rim and some string from which he must adjust his depth perception. Optically this is difficult.

See Diagram 181.

Send your best corner shot down the floor early and have him set up camp in either corner. (It is best to alternate occasionally.) Whichever side he chooses determines placement of the other men.

B will set a low post on the same side as C. This keeps one back line defender from approaching C.

The other F will play forward on the same side as C. This insures that C can be fed down the side.

P will play high or medium.

G will play center line.

In general, get the ball to C by any of the possible routes, Diagram 182.

C should shoot if he is open. If C is not open, P or L or F will be *unless* the zone overshifts, Diagram 183, in which case it is a good idea to leave this pattern (which we call "C" for corner and give it the code name "Charlie"), and go to a third standard zone attack which we call "B" or "Baker" for obvious reasons.

Diagram 181

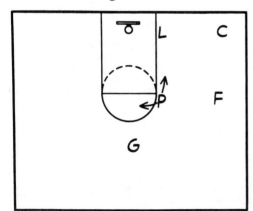

Diagram 182

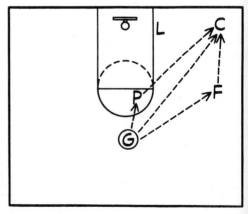

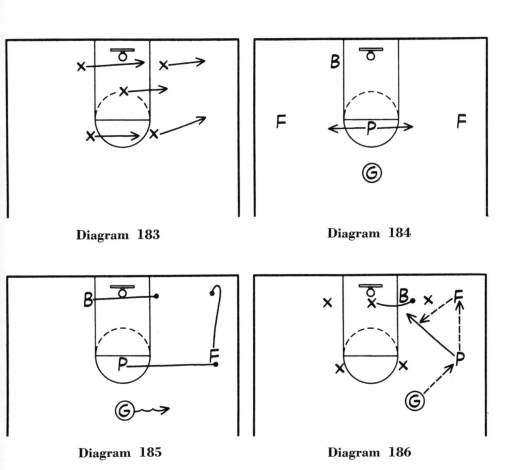

Diagram 183

Diagram 184

Diagram 185

Diagram 186

Charlie is a good zone attack if your corner shooter has the ability to hit and the confidence to shoot it.

Post Wing Offense

B or Baker works best versus a 2-3 defense which resists feeds to the corner via the long pass. Although it can be a continuation of C or Charlie, the following shows it more simplified, Diagram 184.

P is instructed to set a high post, then move to one of the forward positions right or left, at his discretion. If he elects to go to our right, as in Diagram 185, the F on that side clears to the near corner. B plays low post on P's side, G moves over to the same side.

G then feeds P who immediately feeds F in the corner and goes directly at the basket.

81

It is usually easy for F to return the ball immediately to P as in Diagram 186, for an 8 to 10 footer.

If the middle rear man on the zone interrupts P's cut, B is open on the low post for a feed from F. If the front line guard collapses in P's cutting lane, G has moved down into the side forward spot originally played by right F and recently vacated by P, Diagram 187.

Weakside F has three choices. He rebounds weak corner in the shot, comes to the high post from the weakside, balances to the front to replace G, Diagram 188.

As was mentioned earlier, this maneuver can be accomplished from the corner overload game Charlie. Diagram 189 shows the

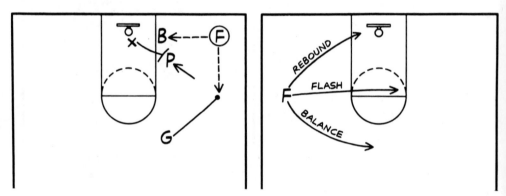

Diagram 187   Diagram 188

first move, then P becomes the replacement for the wing cutter, Diagram 190, as G stays in front.

Baker is a simple little game but it has treated us to a lot of satisfactions.

SINGLE CUTTER DOUBLE POST

A rather popular variation of the 1-3-1 attack is using either the middle guard or a wing forward as a single cutter who moves to the baseline and operates there or in a corner in an attempt to put pressure on the back line, Diagram 191. G feeds, cuts to the baseline and develops an overload on the ball-side.

If G were to feed and go away, Diagram 192, the three-man

triangle would still exist ball-side with (right) F, L, and P, but in addition, better balance would be maintained on the opposite or weakside.

F can feed low post L who goes to a corner to get approximately the same effect, Diagram 193.

Attacking pointed or sharp (one-man front) zones

In order to avoid direct pressure on the ball from the pointed zone, our choice is to use a two-guard offense because the holes are not in the floor center, Diagram 194.

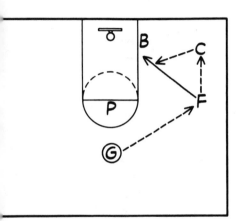

Diagram 189

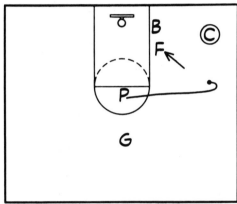

Diagram 190

Diagram 191

Diagram 192

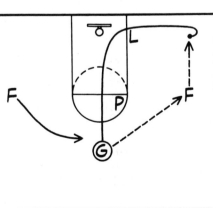

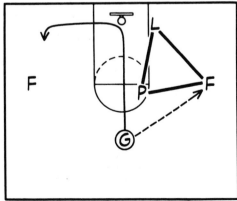

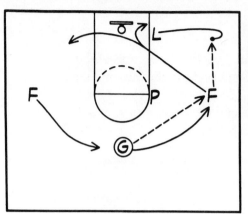

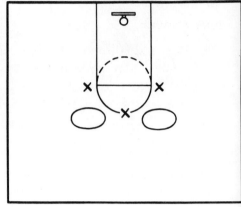

Diagram 193   **Diagram 194**

The best two sharp zone defenses are the 1-3-1 zone and the 1-2-2 or "spearhead."

Attacking the 1-3-1 zone

I very much respect the 1-3-1 zone. Because it can so easily keep three men in line with the ball and basket, cover post men, prevents the ball from advancing down the side yet keeps pressure on the front and covers the corners well *if* played properly, it is usually good for a few fear traumas to the coach who is confronted by it without preparation. I've seen, I'm sure, a greater number of futile strategies versus this zone than against any other. After becoming concerned for my own welfare when this little deal crosses my path some night, I am eternally grateful for a couple of tips from Mark Whiteaker which have since served often to save my neck.

This is the only 1-3-1 attack I've ever needed. It works. See Diagram 195.

> *F men*
>
> 1. Work in and out in their traffic lanes at the positions indicated. Normally you will prefer to be in the number 1 position for feeds directly from G or P, but you may work at number 2 spot if G's get into trouble.
>
> *G men*
>
> 1. Stay dispersed enough so that the front man cannot control you both without movement.

2. First choice to zip the overhead two hand feed directly to either F at a spot near the corner of the board. This feed can go, if practiced well, to the opposite side of F if the goalie respects the near side F too much, Diagram 196.

3. Second choice for G is to feed P at the high post, who immediately pivots and faces in and feeds either F at the number one spots, Diagram 197. P must pivot immediately, and not bounce the ball before doing so!

4. Third choice in case you can't feed F or P is step into the hole and pop, as in Diagram 198.

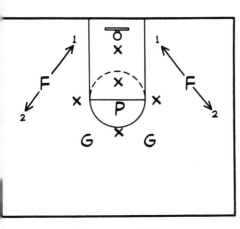

Diagram 195

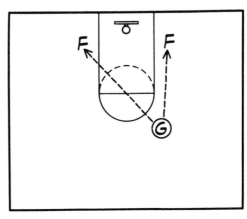

Diagram 196

Diagram 197

Diagram 198

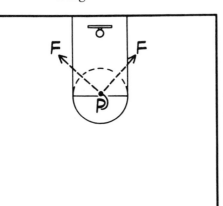

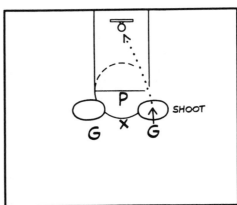

Post

Expect the feed from G even if you must approach the top of the circle to get it. Turn and look for F's (you *can* make this turn with proper footwork described in detail in Chapter 7). If defensive p falls off to cover one F as the goalie takes the other, drive quickly since you will have 3-on-2, Diagram 199, or shoot the 15 foot two-point free throw!

It works.

Attacking the 1-2-2 zone

There isn't a better zone than this 1-2-2 or "spearhead" because

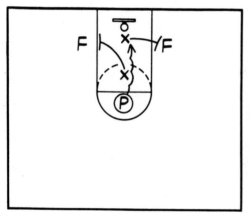

Diagram 199

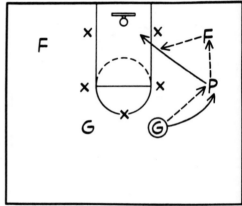

Diagram 200

Diagram 201

Diagram 202

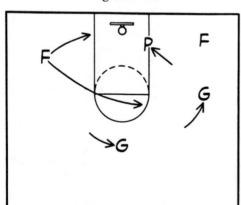

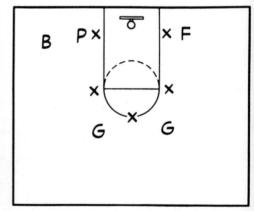

the movement is so effective. It puts a lot of pressure on the ball at all times.

Our preference is to use a variation of our man-to-man attack on it. A standardized attack, namely, a two-guard version of Baker is effective. Diagram 200 shows the first move and Diagram 201 the follow-up.

ROTATING PATTERN VERSUS 1-2-2

Inasmuch as spearhead zones are supposed to be weak on the baseline, there is a continuity pattern which produces a series of screens on the back defensive men for a baserunner who alternates from side to side as the other four players run a four man continuity, Diagram 202. These four continuity men are ball handlers and screeners; B is the shooter.

Diagram 203 shows the action without defense.

G on the side of B feeds B and cuts diagonally through to the opposite low post man. The replaced far low post comes out as the off guard replaces the cutting guard.

Left G's purpose in going through is to screen the defensive man on that side who is probably in the lane directing his attention to the ball in possession of B, Diagram 204. G sets an outside (rearside) screen to keep this man from returning to the right side, because B will soon arrive at this spot, Diagram 205 shows how B does this by feeding left G, who feeds F who is now out, who feeds B behind the new screen.

If no shot, the continuity continues as F cuts to screen at the left low post, as the other two men (front G and now, for the first time, P) rotate out to act as feeders, Diagram 206.

Diagram 203	Diagram 204

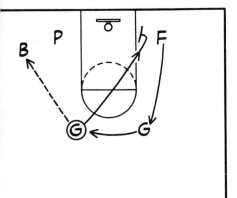 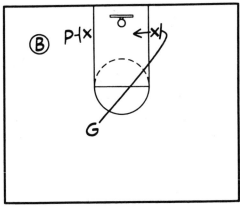

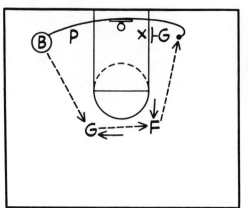

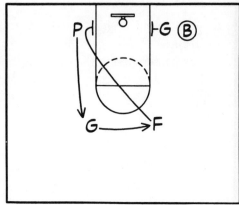

Diagram 205	Diagram 206

The ball comes out now, over and down again behind the new screen as B runs baseline, Diagram 207.

This continuity is simple, yet demands considerable practice. I prefer to rely on a less demanding scheme. It is an excellent ball handling, screen, and baseline-shooting drill. It will produce shots and it does work versus a 1-2-2.

Flash post attack

The 1-2-2 can be attacked by alternately flashing corner posts from a three man (one guard and two wing men) front, Diagram 208, and continuing from side to side, Diagram 209, with perhaps the weakside wing slipping down to rebound or play weakside.

Diagram 207	Diagram 208

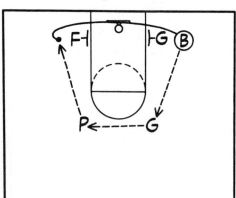

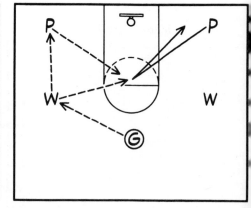

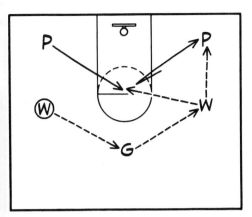

Diagram 209

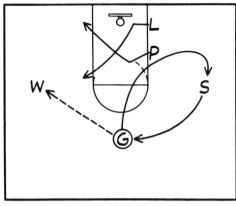

Diagram 210

Trample zone attack

Our stated favorite zone attack is our Trample offense variation of alternating posts. We use this against flat zones most often. The weakside action resembles our 22 man-to-man weakside pattern, Diagram 210. G feeds W, cuts down and away, L and P alternate from low to high and vice versa to the ball, as S balances to the front. W tries to 1) feed the post men, 2) score himself, 3) lob to the new weakside. All men hunt for holes and free lance if easily possible. Diagram 211 shows a repeated cycle.

The strongside or 23 version also is adaptable to zones. The differences in the zone version is that P slides down to become

Diagram 211

Diagram 212

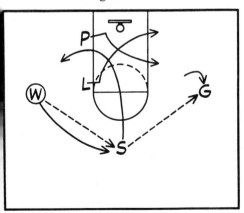

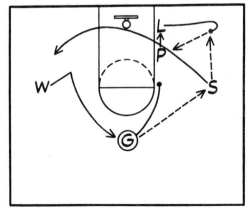

89

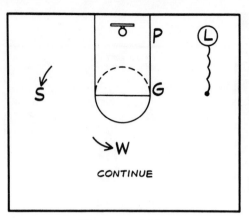

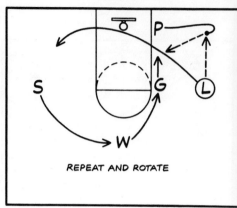

CONTINUE

REPEAT AND ROTATE

Diagram 213

Diagram 214

Diagram 215

Diagram 216

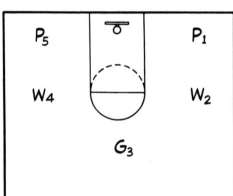

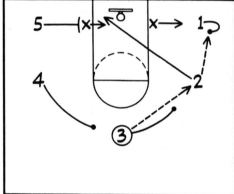

the new low post as G moves to the high post, Diagram 212. This becomes a full five-man rotation as L dribbles out to become the new cutter. Should he feed P coming to the corner, etc., Diagram 213, and Diagram 214 show resemblance to the Baker attack.

Weakside twin post zone attack

If Trample doesn't click versus the zone, the Weakside Twin Post game is next. We have never found a better zone attack. Even though it initially is a one-guard offense, it becomes a two-guard offense *after* the first move. It is, therefore, versatile and can be used against all zones—and we do so, Diagram 215. For sake of clarity, numbers 1 through 5 are used instead of letters.

90

The idea of this game is to move the ball and allow the defense to give attention to it on one side. Usually the defense will move a step or more to the ball or at least turn to face it. A screen is set to keep the rearmost backline man from recovering or returning home from this reaction. A single cutter attempts to shoot from behind this screen as the ball is returned from its side location to the opposite side, i.e., the side to which the cutter goes.

32, SINGLE WING CUTTER

The "32" play is so-called because the right wing, who is numbered 2, is the prime option. Number 3 starts the action by feeding 2, who feeds his baseline mate, 1, and cuts to the opposite side, Diagram 216. If 1 can hit 2 on a give-go, he does so, although he usually cannot.

Number 1 immediately feeds out to 3 who *partially* replaces 2 (3 goes about two-thirds the distance to 2's original spot. Number 4 comes half way to the front (4 and 3 are now in typical two-guard positions). In the meantime 5 sets a screen on the edge of the lane on his near defender who has probably turned or drifted to the ball. Number 2 quickly goes under 5's screen, faces the basket and gets ready to receive the ball for the eight foot baseline shot over the screen. We believe we can return the ball to 2 before the defense can recover, Diagram 217.

In summary:

1. Ball to baseline, cutter go away
2. Far man set rear screen as front men semi-rotate
3. Immediately ball comes out of baseline to far side, usually with three passes, zip, zip, zip

If the defense overplays on 3 and/or 4, we may go to the lob, Diagram 218, or the lob may be used by 3 as a short cut, Diagram 219.

If the rear defensive man whom 5 attempts to screen escapes the screen, 5 may be open inside him and the feed then goes to 5 instead of 2, Diagram 220.

In addition, all hands are hunting for holes. Numbers 4 and 3, especially, are able to penetrate for the 10 or 11 foot jumper at the top and sides, Diagram 221.

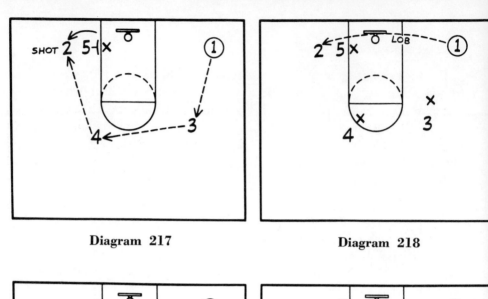

Diagram 217

Diagram 218

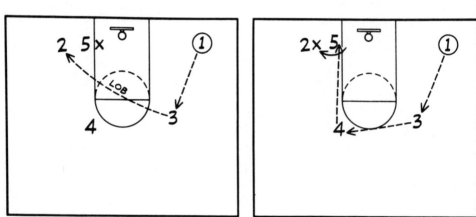

Diagram 219

Diagram 220

Diagram 221

Diagram 222

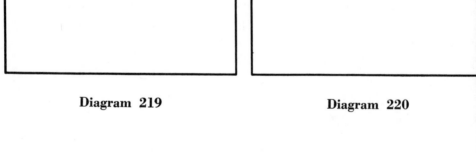

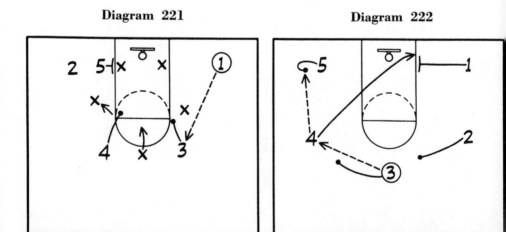

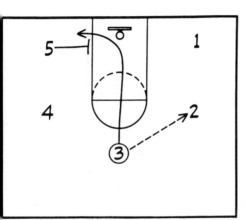

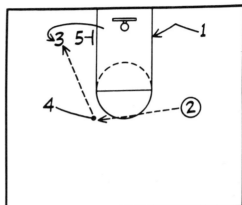

Diagram 223   **Diagram 224**

Should the guard initially feed left to 4, the play would be 34, as number 4 is the cutter-shooter, Diagram 222.

33, SINGLE GUARD CUTTER

The same play effect is 33 or the 3 man cutting and shooting, Diagram 223. This is a quicker play than 34 or 32 because the ball does *not* go first to the baseline. It returns in two passes instead of three, Diagram 224. Number 3 merely feeds and cuts *away* from the side to which he fed. The cue or signal that 33 rather than 32 is on is the cut by 3. If 3 feeds and cuts, 33 is on. If 3 feeds 2 and *stands,* then 32 is on and 2 will cut.

Diagram 225   **Diagram 226**

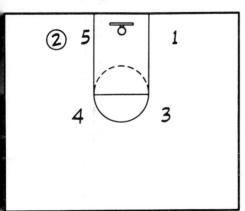

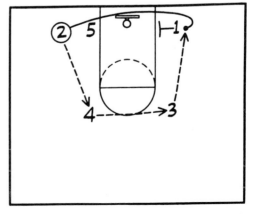

If 32, 33, or 34 is run and no shot results, an overload has been established, Diagram 225. This overload can be unloaded in the same manner as described for the Rotating Pattern, diagrams 202 through 207. The 1, 3, 4, and 5 men can also remain relatively stationary and not rotate, but merely feed around the horn to 2 coming out on the far side behind 1's screen, Diagram 226.

SEVEN

Conducting Practice
Sessions to Teach Offense

Scrimmage

Players would scrimmage every minute of practice if allowed. Only games are more fun than scrimmaging. Scrimmages are vital in the first three to four weeks of organized team practice. After this initial period in which players become accustomed to each other, the total game, game situations, and develop a respect and an appreciation for perfection in the myriad fundamentals, we feel scrimmaging should be minimized.

In the short time available, the basketball coach has literally dozens of essential skills, vital strategies, do's and don'ts, etc. that must be taught each boy. If perfection or even a moderate degree of development is sought in each of these specifics, then the one and one-half hour available daily is hardly enough to find time to scrimmage often or long. This approach presupposes that each skill, each strategy, each understanding must be 1) lectured about, 2) demonstrated, 3) practiced repetitiously, 4) mused over and concentrated attention given thereto. Some coaches feel that the best way—the only way—this can be achieved is in actual playing situations. These coaches will scrimmage most of the time. Many such coaches are highly successful, perhaps in spite of, if not because of, this approach.

If specific tasks are worked on in practice sessions with no other detracting elements present, the player will be "ready" and "fresh" when game time arrives. In summary, I tend to feel that too-frequent scrimmaging is a rather sure-fire short cut to staleness and inefficient learning and development of perfection in fundamentals.

"If you want to have some fun, boys, you'll have it on game night," which does *not* mean practice sessions will be dull or boring. It does mean your best play of the week will not have occurred on Wednesday night's practice floor.

I don't like to scrimmage . . . much. Early in the year, yes. After that, occasionally, yes. Long, frequent scrimmages, no!

Drills

Drills for drill's sake are no good. If a drill definitely and directly serves and accomplishes a specific objective, e.g., teaches a boy how to keep possession of a ball when confronted by two aggressive double-teaming opponents, then okay. Each and every drill must *directly* serve a specific need. Each drill must be simple. It must be interesting. It must be of short duration. It must be the best known way to develop skill or knowledge of fitness in players.

We try to keep our drills minimal in number. In general, we have about one good drill for each skill area of basketball. We repeat these regularly; depend on them. We do not want to be "teaching how to drill." If a boy learns a drill as a freshman, he will (probably) be using it for the next three years. We expect to say "Okay, men, Wheeling for three minutes," and immediately get full action by every man on deck. No questions or confusion such as "Uh, coach, is that the one where . . . ?"

Fundamentals

How many essential fundamentals are there in this game of basketball? About a dozen? Several dozen? Hundreds? The following treatment of drills, a drill for each basic fundamental is one interpretation of what fundamentals are vital and therefore necessary—and those which are not!

My Favorite Drill, "Wheeling"

If a boy can execute this drill, he can play basketball. If taught properly, any normal boy can do this drill. If a boy isn't already an accomplished basketball player, this drill will do more for him than any other single drill I know. If I were limited to using only one drill for my players, players of any size or ability, it would be this drill, "Wheeling."

"Wheeling" is a one-on-one drill. Start with ball possession about 15 feet from the basket, back to the basket facing out. The ball is held in both hands, feet in a parallel stance, Diagram 227.

Wheeling develops: 1) ball handling, 2) confidence, 3) footwork, 4) jump shooting, 5) driving and lay-up shooting, 6) dribbling, 7) defensive skills—for the defensive man.

Specifically, it develops a boy's ability to successfully execute the most difficult of all offensive tasks, namely: starting from a back-to-the-basket position, and taking a ball to the basket and scoring. In accomplishing this, the following specific skills are developed: 1) pivoting right or left, 2) facing an opponent, who is very close, with confidence that he cannot take the ball from you or cause you to lose it, 3) driving right and/or left (to both the weak and strong side), 4) dribbling right and/or left, 5) protecting oneself and the ball from defensive pressure enroute, 6) reacting to defensive reaction and appropriate alteration of options (ability to reverse routes), 7) faking drive and recovering to jump or set shoot.

In addition, Wheeling does more for post men than other players. It therefore makes all your players capable of playing post, a desirable skill, I believe. Here are the teaching cues to Wheeling.

Starting from the 15 foot spot, the player should only slightly crouch, just enough to unlock the knees and feel comfortable. He may go right or left, the example, Diagram 228, will be to the right. Lift the right foot, pivoting on the left, and after turning, place the right foot in a position: a. flat on the floor; b. pointing directly at basket; c. at least even with, but preferably six inches beyond the defender's outside foot; d. as near laterally to the defender's foot as possible so that e. most of the body's weight is shifted to this right foot—slam it down hard on the floor.

The entire body is now facing the basket, the ball is held in both hands near the navel, the offensive man is in a low crouch

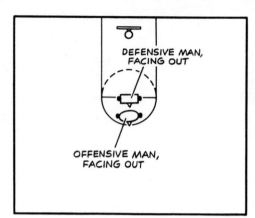

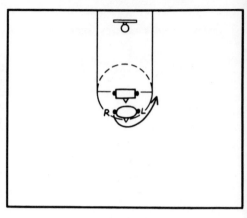

Diagram 227   **Diagram 228**

with a long extended right leg, Diagram 229. If the player can see the floor just to the outside of his opponent's (left) heel, he can put his right foot down on that spot. The tendency is to step far to the right of the defender, Diagram 230. We call this "driving to the cheerleaders' bench," and we don't allow it.

If the foot is slammed heavily to the floor, the weight will tend to be on it and if the weight is mainly on it, the power to shove off it (reverse and go opposite) will be there if this need arises. Also, if the weight is on it and the route ahead is clear, the player's body will naturally follow in a controlled fall in this direction.

If the player can *see* the floor at spot "x," Diagram 231, he can drive through the spot and subsequently on to the basket. Therefore, unless the defender has jumped or slid back to a position over x spot, the offensive player can merely *drop* the ball slightly outside of this spot (no need to dribble it, just drop it and it will dribble itself the first time!), then, and only then, raise the rear (pivot) foot and run to the basket, perhaps with one or two more

Diagram 229   **Diagram 230**

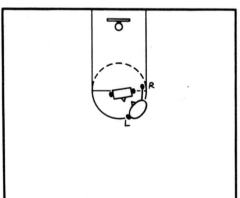

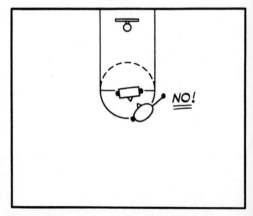

bounces (dribbles) with the outside hand. We refer to this move as the "wheel left, drive right" inasmuch as the pivot turn is to the left side of the body (counterclockwise) and after turning, the drive is to the right side.

Key points in the movement are: use a crossover pivot (right foot crosses over the left); step as *close* to the opponent's left foot as possible; step as deeply as possible past the defender before dribbling, losing balance, or moving the pivot foot.

- The second possibility in Wheeling is a built-in alternate move in case the defender appears suddenly in the path of the wheel man, on the x spot. See Diagram 232. If this defensive reaction to the wheel occurs, the wheeler can see it by the time his right foot is ready to slam down. He slams it down in the same (approximate) spot, transfers his weight to it as usual (remember that where the weight is one's power is also), and instantly exerts a powerful thrust down through the floor at this right foot which tends to transfer his weight back to his left, rear foot. The wheeler immediately raises his right foot and places it heavily and harshly (slam!) on the *left* side of his opponent, Diagram 233. This dual step with the right foot "slam right to the right," slam right to the left" can usually be accomplished before or in less time than the defender needs to readjust back to the wheeler's left (defender's right). Wheeler, of course, attempts to step close to and deeply beyond defender with this "second side" move, just as he did on his initial step to the first or right side. Wheeler then drops the ball to the floor at his left hip and with one left-hand bounce is at the board. Players are quick to appreciate the ease with

Diagram 231   **Diagram 232**

which they are able to dribble left-handed as they come out of this move. This "move to the second side" or "wheel left, drive left" is best versus an opponent who reacts quickly to fakes or quick movement. It is also the best move for protection of the ball in the dribble because the right leg is extended between the ball and the man.

A third possibility is to be used versus a defender who does react sufficiently to stop both the first and second moves. The wheeler fakes the first side, then fakes the second side, then steps (retreats) about 24 inches with the right (slam) foot and puts this foot down quickly under his own body, slightly advanced to his own left foot, Diagram 234. The wheeler is now in shooting position facing the basket and can jump shoot, usually before the defender can advance on him, Diagram 235.

Fourth, fifth, and sixth options are to repeat the first, second and third moves *if* the defender advances (recovers) too fast back into the face of the wheeler as the third move is completed.

There are three offensive threats as the offensive man wheels left (first side, second side, step back and shoot). There are three mirrored moves as he wheels right, crossing his left foot over his right as he turns clockwise, slamming his left foot in three different spots. These "wheel left" options seem less natural at first, but in a short time are as easily executed as the left wheel. The move to the second side in wheel left is a real "natural" as the ball goes down on the dribble with the right hand plus protection of the left extended leg. Try it. Teach all your boys to wheel. No defender will ever hold them cold. You'll also have a squad full of boys who can operate on the post.

Diagram 233	Diagram 234
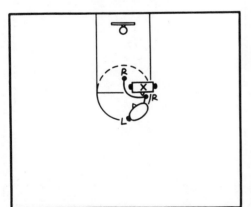	

Skills learned from this one drill

Ball Handling

This is inherent as wheeler learns he can move the ball about in front of the defender and if he moves it quickly enough he can retain it. In fact, if defender tends to give too much attention to the ball he is apt to go off balance and become vulnerable to the drive.

Confidence

No greater value could emerge for a player than to know he can now, from a rear facing position, turn and look any opponent eye to eye and move on him.

Footwork

Weight shifting, quick and *hard* stepping educate a player in regard to his balance and ability to shake defenders.

Jump Shooting

Although this wheeling drill is not the only jump shot predecessor, the opportunity to jump shoot in rapid sequence with other scoring threats makes for better jump shooting.

Driving

Four possibilities are always available as wheeler comes to recognize them.

Diagram 235   **Diagram 236**

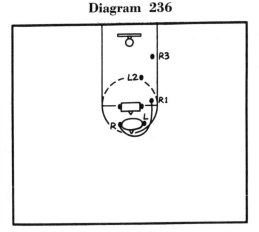

Dribbling

Because the wheeler is down low and in a forward lean after he completes his turn, dribbling is simplified and he has frequent opportunity to blend weak and strong hand dribbling with weak and strongside footwork, the two basic essentials of any "floor" man.

Defense

Defenders' experience moves quickly to their right and left as well as delayed to either side as they move rearward and laterally. They also get a chance to react to the jump shot.

In review of wheeling, there are three choices in Wheel Left:

1. Wheel left, drive right, Diagram 236
2. Wheel left, drive left, Diagram 237
3. Wheel left, step back and pop, Diagram 238

There are three choices in Wheel Right:

1. Wheel right, drive left, Diagram 239
2. Wheel right, drive right, Diagram 240
3. Wheel right, step back and pop, Diagram 241

Pattern (team) drills to teach pattern play

If our teams pattern well it is because we give a considerable bit of attention to this. We get more results by 3 to 5 minutes of pattern drill daily than by 30 to 50 minutes of scrimmaging. Each of our offensive patterns has a number. These drills teach pattern recognition, movement routes, movement cues, screen assignments, floor balance, passing, etc. They are *not* intended to be shooting drills.

21 Drill

Several times each week, we open the non-shooting phase of practice sessions with this: "Five men at the west basket in 21, run six cycles then shoot, 3 minutes." If our Twin Tandem Post game weave is our 21 game, we would weave six exchanges and then pop in a shot, quickly regroup and repeat until three minutes pass, Diagram 242. There is, of course, no defense.

22 Drill

22 is the weakside Trample game. Daily we drill 22 for 3 to 5

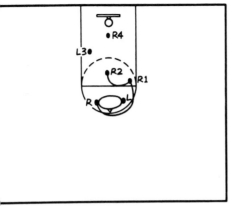

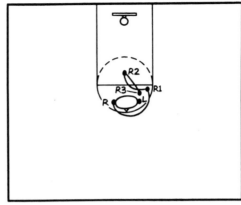

Diagram 237   Diagram 238

Diagram 239   Diagram 240

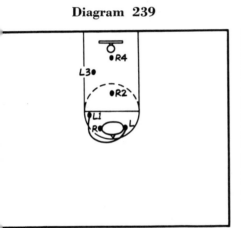

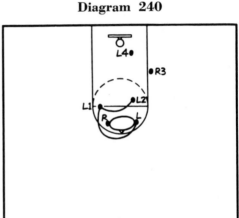

minutes. "22 for five cycles, then shoot from the top of the key" means of course that only after five complete cycles will the shot be taken, then they will be checked to see if they balance 3 1/2 properly, Diagram 243.

23 Drill

23 is Strongside Trample, and the same procedure is followed as in 22, Diagram 244. About 50 repetitions can be accomplished in 5 minutes, many, many times the number in 50 minutes of scrimmage.

24 Drill

Should 24 be the post split game of the Trample, we would do

103

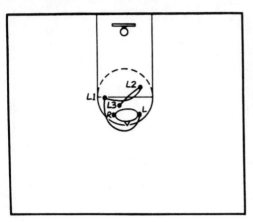

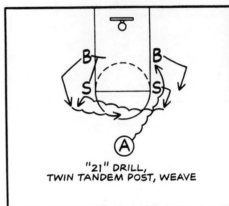

"21" DRILL,
TWIN TANDEM POST, WEAVE

Diagram 241

Diagram 242

Diagram 243

Diagram 244

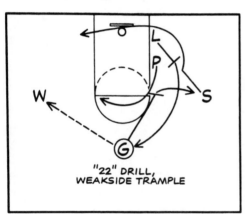

"22" DRILL,
WEAKSIDE TRAMPLE

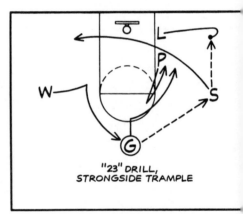

"23" DRILL,
STRONGSIDE TRAMPLE

just this for about 4 minutes and shoot perhaps every cycle or perhaps every 8th one, Diagram 245.

50 Drill

The Weakside Twin Post is 50. We run through all the options, usually with orders to shoot only after going so far, for example, the eleventh option, Diagram 246.

Our zone attacks are usually given a 30 series number. If we are interested in sharpening up on our assignments in 32, the single cutter pattern, we might say "32 for 2 minutes, lob from 3 and shoot," or we may want our front guards to get practice in hunting for holes; then it would be "32, hunt for holes 3 and 4 shoot."

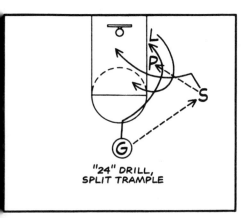

"24" DRILL,
SPLIT TRAMPLE

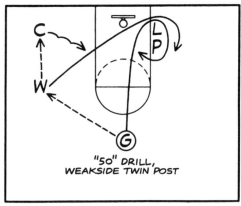

"50" DRILL,
WEAKSIDE TWIN POST

Diagram 245   **Diagram 246**

30 Drill

This is our basic attack versus 1-3-1 and we shoot from the "spots" or holes, Diagram 247.

31 Drill

31 is the number assigned to Baker attack. We would usually use only three men on half court and three more doing likewise on the other side, Diagram 248. This keeps twice the number of men busy.

32 Drill

This is merely a no-defense five-man zone pattern drill as described above. In Diagram 249 the shot is taken from the baseline screen by 2.

33 Drill

The 3 man cutter shoots as his teammates screen, feed and rebound his shot, Diagram 250.

34 Drill

By this means we learn to unload the overload developed by running a 32 or a 33. We usually 34 it several times before shooting, again with the idea of giving all five men an opportunity to run through every position so that recognition and appreciation of each assignment is developed, Diagram 251.

In summary, these pattern drills are designed to *"learn"* (rather than teach!) the men the patterns through fast and frequent repetition.

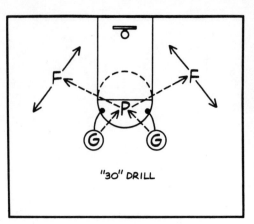

F
F
P
G
G
"30" DRILL

Diagram 247

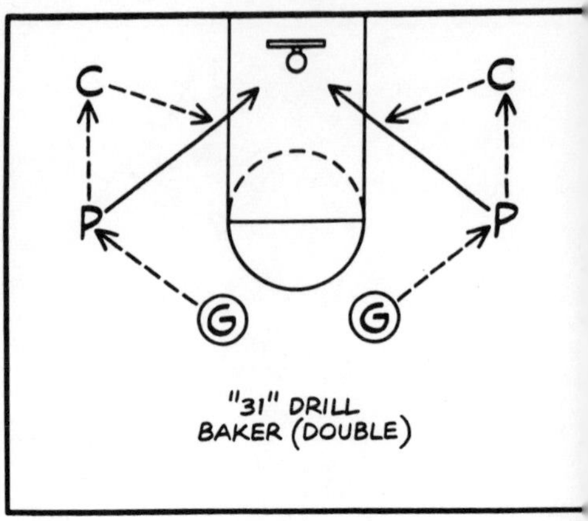

C
C
P
P
G
G
"31" DRILL
BAKER (DOUBLE)

Diagram 248

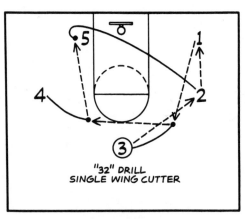

5
1
4
2
3
"32" DRILL
SINGLE WING CUTTER

Diagram 249

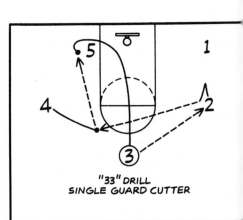

5
1
4
2
3
"33" DRILL
SINGLE GUARD CUTTER

Diagram 250

Diagram 251

2
5
1
4
3
"34" DRILL
ROTATION OR UNLOADING

Diagram 252

X
W
S
S
S
S
S
S
G
MANAGER
"COME-UNDER" DRILL

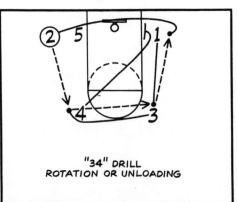

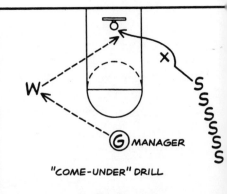

Shooting drills

The first twenty minutes of each practice session is spent on individual shooting. Whenever there is a need to check on our shooting exactly as we get shots in our patterns, we use pattern segment shooting drills. We seldom use any "shooting drills," such as a 21 point game, etc. All shooting drills must be taken from the context of one of our patterns. In this way we practice the timing, feeding and reception, use of screens, etc., exactly as it will develop in our patterns. This enhances the pattern as well as develops shooting.

In shooting drills, we are after snappy but accurate shooting. We want to get a million shots in a few minutes and make them all. If we ever condone fooling around in practice, it certainly is *not* during shooting practice.

PATTERN SEGMENTS TO TEACH SHOOTING

Diagram 252 indicates how we drill our come-under shot in the Trample. All players except one (W) play strongside and come to the basket over a pseudo screen at x. W feeds hairline high briskly, S comes back into the board with all his weight, rebounds his own ball and feeds out to the manager. Do this right and left sides. Change the W feeder every 20 feeds.

Diagram 253 indicates the "come-up" move by the low post after screening S. Everyone plays low post except one W feeder who is changed every 20 to 25 feeds. L rebounds his own and quickly returns to the same line. The main thing is for L to get quickly into shooting position before the ball arrives.

Diagram 254 shows the lob from W over to G at the new weakside. W must keep the trajectory moderate; G shoots instantly and rebounds his own. It is a good principle that whenever possible, shooters follow and rebound their own, stuffing all missed shots in on the follow-up.

The strongside give-go can best be learned well by a 23 drill segment as in Diagram 255. A manager can rebound and feed out to another boy who keeps the S men supplied.

Typical weakside Twin Post segment shooting is shown in figures 256, 257, 258, and 259. It is easy and desirable to practice each pattern option as a drill. This is the ultimate method of get-

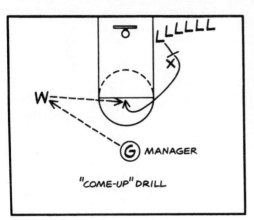

LLLLLL

W

MANAGER

"COME-UP" DRILL

Diagram 253

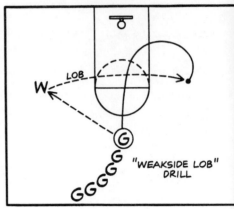

LOB

W

"WEAKSIDE LOB" DRILL

Diagram 254

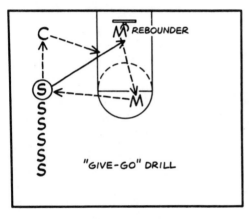

C

REBOUNDER

S

M

"GIVE-GO" DRILL

Diagram 255

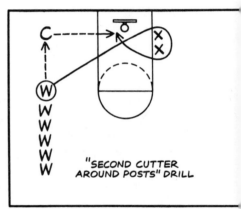

C

W

"SECOND CUTTER AROUND POSTS" DRILL

Diagram 256

Diagram 257

Diagram 258

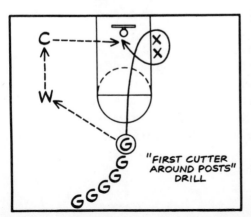

C

W

"FIRST CUTTER AROUND POSTS" DRILL

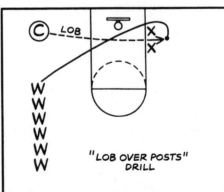

C   LOB

W

"LOB OVER POSTS" DRILL

"DRIVING OVER THE POSTS"
DRILL

Diagram 259

"JUMP SHOOTING OVER SCREENS"
DRILL

Diagram 260

ting the most *efficiency* into your practice schedule. These are merely examples.

JUMP SHOOTING OVER SCREENS

Because of the relative importance of both jump shooting and setting and using (shooting properly over) screens, we believe that about 3 or 4 minutes nearly every night should be spent doing this. Two men pair up. The screener takes the ball, goes to any spot 10 to 30 feet out, faces out and holds the ball for the shooter to take from him. The shooter gets about 3 to 5 feet away from the screener, shoots directly over his head, breaks quickly to either side to rebound his own shot before it hits the floor, if possible, dribbles to a new spot. The original screener follows quickly and becomes the new shooter, Diagram 260. Continue; hurry and don't miss! Screeners usually take the ball to one of the shooter's favorite spots.

HIGH SPEED LAY-UPS

We like to conclude each practice session with this simple but demanding drill. Each man has a ball. He drives at sprint speed to a basket, slows up only on his last step and lays it in. Alternate hands each time, Diagram 261. *Full* speed, make 10 and shower.

SPEED SHOOTING

There seems to be some value in practice shooting hurriedly at a pace just short of "rushing." One man rebounds as a buddy pops from outside, changes location by at least a step, is fed and fires again. One minute and change jobs. Compare results. Don't over-do this, but it has value in creating enthusiasm, drilling for

109

desperation moments in games, and teaching shooters that they often don't have "all day" to shoot, Diagram 262.

It is also good to operate this as a one-man drill as the shooter retrieves his own shot and hurries to the outside to repeat, etc.

Preliminary Practice Shooting

Each practice begins with each boy, with his own personal ball, trotting a couple of laps to get "into the swing." He then starts close (short) shots of any type that suits him, then, as his fine shooting muscles, tendons and ligaments loosen and warm (and *not before!*) he lengthens the shooting distance to his long shots. We do not permit a cold man to shoot long shots. Beyond these couple of limitations, the players are coached very little during this shooting period. They shoot! We offer suggestions if asked and correct only obviously severe defects, but mainly they shoot. They don't scrimmage one-on-one, two-on-two, visit, goof-off: They *shoot!* Twenty minutes. Every day.

"Drag"

This is a technique which is employed in support of the wheeling drill. Dragging develops ball handling, moving, and shooting. We use it mainly as a means of getting a shot, a board shot which is either a lay-up or short hook-lay-up. It is used from a face out position at the post when the defensive man is skin-to-skin and too close to allow the "wheel," Diagram 263.

The left foot slides left as far as possible (the lower the stance, the longer the step), then the right foot follows in a shuffling slide. The ball is dribbled with the right hand just in advance of

Diagram 261

Diagram 262

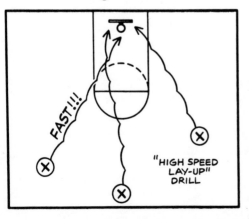

"HIGH SPEED LAY-UP" DRILL

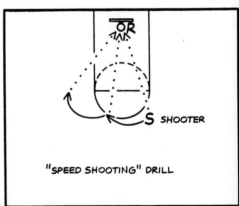

"SPEED SHOOTING" DRILL

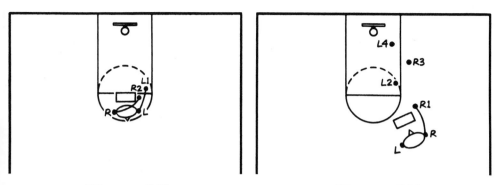

Diagram 263   Diagram 264

the dragging, trailing (right) foot. Two or three step-together, step-togethers, one bounce for each and the offensive man can go down to the board. He may reverse and go opposite so long as his dribble isn't interrupted; no turning is necessary as he continues to face out. He turns one quarter turn at the board and shoots outside hand, or if he is large and can hook, he may. Dragging is a poor substitute for the wheel. I hate to see basketball players try to play as they look at the basket with their gluteals. It is a valuable skill to have ready, however, versus a close-riding rear defense.

ROCKER DRILL

Second only to wheeling in importance is the rocker maneuver. It is the primary movement used to drive past a defender as the offensive man starts from a face-the-basket position.

It is, in essence, identical to wheeling after the pivot turn has been made. The right-hand man will step right with a hard foot slam, close to and beyond the left side of the defender. If the offensive man can see the deck unobstructed (which should allow him freedom to get his head and shoulders beyond the defender, thus imposing major liability for ensuing contact on the defender as per the rule book), he drops the dribble down and drives right, Diagram 264. This we refer to as "going right to the open (or first) side."

If the defender cuts off the driving lane, the right foot is quickly slammed a second time to the opposite (left) side and the ball is dropped down for a left-hand dribble since then the left foot (pivot foot) is removed and the movement is to the basket, Diagram 265. This is going right to the closed or second side, the

111

preferred side on which to drive on any defender because the ball is protected by the extended adjacent leg alongside the defender.

This rocker skill must be learned both *right* (open and closed, or if you will, open step side and crossing step side, stepping with the right foot) and *left* to the first and second, or open and closed, or open and crossover, step side. Diagram 266 shows going left to the crossover or second side; Diagram 267 shows the left rocker to the first or open side.

Ball handling drills

In order to give offensive men the confidence and poise needed to work against an aggressive man-to-man defender we tell them that "no one, not even a better man, can take the ball away from you if you will use a few simple techniques." We mean it, we believe this is a true statement. Here are the guidelines an offensive man keeps in mind to realize success versus a defender who comes up close determined to steal the ball.

ONE-ON-ONE KEEP AWAY DRILL

1. Crouch and look him eye to eye, face him.
2. Ball in both hands, do *not* dribble or reverse away from him, feet parallel and shoulder width.
3. If he reaches in, hold ball between your two ankles and 3 inches off floor. Your arms will be straight as you reach back and keep your eyes on his eyes, your head up.
4. If he reaches in to the ball, twist ball a quarter turn, this will roll his arm into your forearms and cut his touch off removing his hand from ball.
5. If he is longer armed than you or if he gets off balance, use a forward pivot with one leg and step through (up and laterally) his arm with your leg. This will remove his arm and hand from the ball.
6. Immediately pivot again with the same foot and return to a front position *facing* him, being reluctant to staying in a reverse position.
7. Remember to keep head up, ball three inches off floor and between your two ankle knobs.
8. If you are double-teamed, the fast pivot cut-offs will keep both men from grasping the ball.

This drill will prove to the offensive man that he can maintain

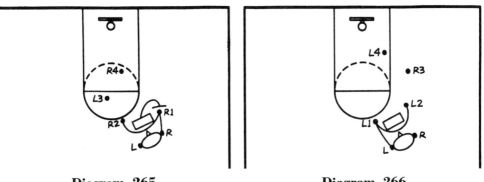

Diagram 265   Diagram 266

possession and control *without* turning tail (reverse facing) and *without* dribbling (fleeing!). He now has learned he can play the game and face the basket at all times he so desires.

Lob

This lob has been described as a moderately arched pass that drops the ball over the intervening defenders to a spot. The simple learning procedure is to put a receiver between two defenders, each about 10 to 15 feet front and rear. The passer then attempts to arch the ball to the receiver between the defenders, Diagram 268. Too flat and D 1 deflects or intercepts, too much arch and both D 1 and D 2 move to intercept it on descent.

Two Hand Overhead Pass

The values of using this as our basic pass are:

1. Greatest accuracy potential. The pass is made from a position near the vision line and sighting, aiming, space and depth judgments are easier and more reliable than a ball started from elsewhere.
2. Two hands over the head are more flexible than two hands from the waist because the elbows are less restricted. Try it!
3. Ball is higher above floor and thus can be thrown directly in line or even downward without the need for the first half of the trajectory route—the ball is already up. Result is shorter flight time.
4. Two hands from this position are able to start and withhold (fake) a pass if danger threatens.
5. Ball can be thrown hard and/or fast if so desired—power is available.

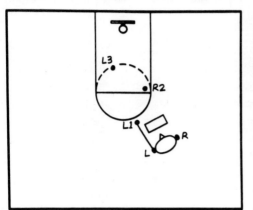

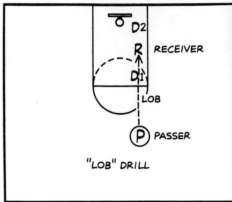

| Diagram 267 | Diagram 268 |

6. Easily jump shot with minimal pre-movement.
7. Moves the ball above the normal hand height of defensive men.
8. Little preparatory movement (windup) required—pass can be "gotten away" quickly.

Two hand passing from the overhead position is somewhat unnatural at first. Two men should stand ten feet apart and from a front-rear staggered foot stance (for forward rearward stability) pass forehead hairline to forehead hairline for 1 or 2 minutes. Remembering to: take a short step forward with the front foot; both hands equal on the ball, no spin, throw a dead ball, Diagram 269.

Each man then steps back one long step and within 5 minutes all your men will be able to pass sideline to sideline (50 feet). Repeat daily for three or four days and they'll have it!

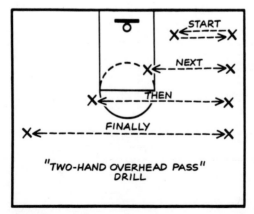

Diagram 269

LONG BOMB

For long distance feeding, especially for cheap fast break feeds, we *practice* how to get the ball down the floor from one end to another. This drill has given us an average of about four extra points per game for several seasons.

Rather than try to throw a bullet from end A to end B, Diagram 270, we want G, out of bounds to feed F, far downcourt and *going* with a pass that 1) comes to within inches of the ceiling and 2) drops in dead center of far free throw circle at X.

This pass will:

1. go over all intervening interceptors.
2. be soft enough for F to handle (how many bullet passes go right on into the far wall or are muffed by F?).

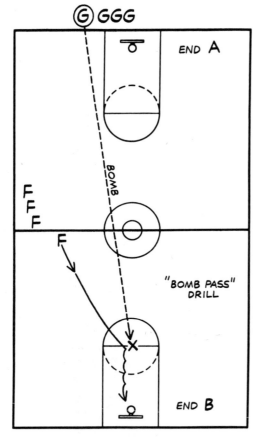

Diagram 270

3. if missed by F, will bounce high and hang up in the general vicinity of our (far end) basket and can be easily pulled down and shot.
4. if intercepted, ball is still at far end and not an immediate threat.
5. remove all indecision and doubt, if used as our primary long feed and usually exclusively to other long passes, as to "where shall G throw?" and "where shall F expect the ball to be?" Everyone of us knows the ball will come down in the circle. Be there.

This looks like an accidental, spontaneous play. Not so. We practice it—it is not so simple that practice is unnecessary—and we are rewarded in points.

Part II

Disciplined
Man-to-Man Defense

EIGHT

Changing from Offense

to Defense

There are no two bedfellows
more compatible than ball control pattern play and highly organized disciplined defense. In fact, ball control pattern play cannot succeed fully unless accompanied by solid defense whereas
disciplined defense goes well with any offensive plan. The effectiveness of any defense is highly dependent upon the rapidity
and effectiveness of changing from offense to defense. This transition period is vital to defensive success. Teams which lack this
ability will never be relative champs.

This discussion involves making the complete change, when it
begins and ends, and how to organize it. This transition proceeds
by phases and these phases are identified and analyzed.

Effective transition from offense to defense is more important
than pattern play itself and is the essential factor which determines
whether an opponent plays "their" game or "our" game!

When defense begins

Defense begins the instant the shot leaves the shooter's hand
and all hands immediately start to balance 3 1/2 as described in
Diagram 89. The tendency is to wait longer before balancing

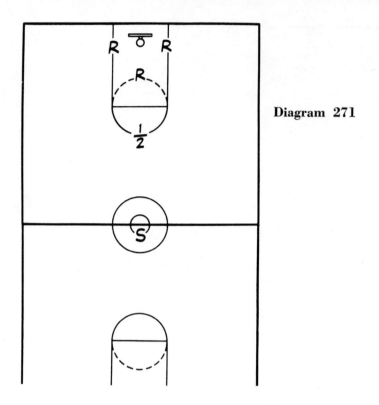

Diagram 271

begins. If balancing doesn't begin until the ball is obtained by the opponents (defense) it is too late—too late for good defense and too late to retrieve the offensive ball for sustained offense.

Balancing

The 3 1/2 offensive balance cup, Diagram 271, described in Chapter 2, is a defensive scheme with offensive tendencies. This is an ideal way to regain possession of the shot basketball before it becomes the property of the opponents. If it is possessed by them, this balance alignment is the best medicine for keeping defensive pressure on the ball.

"Floor balance" is considered vital by some coaches. We tend to belittle symmetrical or "even" floor coverage because we usually find our opponents located about where we are and if we're out of balance, so are they.

OFFENSIVE REBOUNDING

Three men get priority zone-like positions on the board as de-

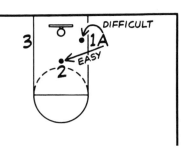 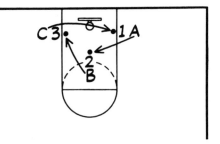

Diagram 272   **Diagram 273**

scribed in Diagram 89, Chapter 2, and await descent of the ball. If we find it difficult to get position, we sometimes cross or switch under the boards. If the opponents are stacked in a triangle, 1-2-3, and we emerge outside them, it is easier for offensive A to get inside on 2 than on 1, Diagram 272. C would go to the inside of 1 as B tried to roll inside 3, Diagram 273.

Another method of switching on rebounds is for all men to rotate toward the corner or balance nearest the shot as in Diagram 274.

We do not encourage offensive tipping, preferring to have the rebounder muscle it back in with two hands, or feed or drive it out to begin offense again. Should we ever have large men we might change this belief.

GETTING BACK AND APPLICATION OF PRESSURE

If the ball is lost to the defensive opponents at the shot, S hustles to a spot directly under the front edge of the defensive rim, Diagram 275. He may, of course, go for interceptions if he can get to the ball, but his safe assignment is to protect the rim. S (safety) is under general orders to: 1) never "take-on" an opponent out in the open floor if you are the last man back on defense because he is an odds-on favorite to drive past you and advance. Instead, 2) always retreat, apparently defending him, feigning stabs at the balls ... "He may cough it up to you." ... but ultimately determined to be between him and any part of the basket as he arrives at or near the board. We will take away the lay-up and give up the outside shot.

Communicating and stopping the ball

S talks to his nearest teammate, 2 (who will be in front of S), to "stop the ball, stop the ball." This means that this second man

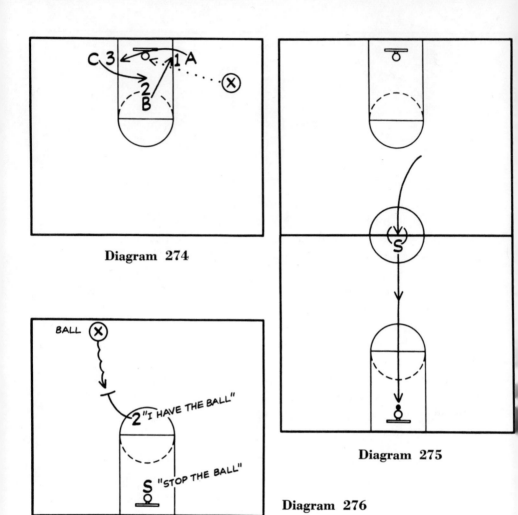

Diagram 274

Diagram 275

Diagram 276

or stopper can be more aggressive. His task is to cause the rapid advance to be halted, slowed, or the ball passed, such pass being liable to interception if near S, Diagram 276.

Getting lost

If after balancing and losing the ball any of us are unable to find the man we are assigned to defend, the "lost" rule is: "Sprint to the defensive end, stand on the dotted circle half, Diagram 277, and search with eyes for your opponent." If he is loose he will sooner or later arrive near here (the basket). He will find you!

If you are lost, get lost at *home!*

122

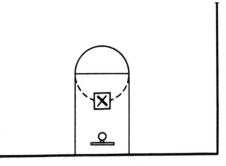

Diagram 277

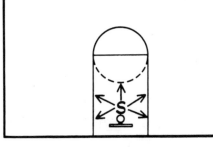

Diagram 278

Protecting the rim and being outnumbered

S never leaves his home spot, which is a tiny spot directly under the front edge of the rim, if he is outnumbered offensively. He must keep one foot on this spot. He can thus step about five feet in all directions to prevent board shots and passes under the basket to the opposite side, Diagram 278.

S must never allow a driving or reaching lay-up to go into the "groove" between the corner of the board and the side edge of the rim, Diagram 279.

There must be no access to the bare board. If a shot is obtained, it must be into or over the body of S, even if a four inch lay-up.

S must assume this one man zone defense and also play defensive quarterback until the last teammate arrives. In any case, he must hook up with the deepest man or man nearest the basket regardless of to whom this opponent is assigned until he is released of this coverage.

If S and 2 are back versus one man, S stays home and 2 locks up very aggressively man-to-man on the one opponent. If two offensive men confront S and 2, the defense is man-to-man and S leaves his spot to do his share.

If, however, 2 and S are outnumbered three to two, they observe the following rules: 1) always play tandem, Diagram 280, never dual (side by side), in a two-man sliding zone. 2 will pressure the ball when it is in front and S will play goalie. 2) on a feed to either side, S slides two steps sideward with two assignments in mind: a) Don't allow the ball to go into the groove between you and the board corner. This means respect the baseline

123

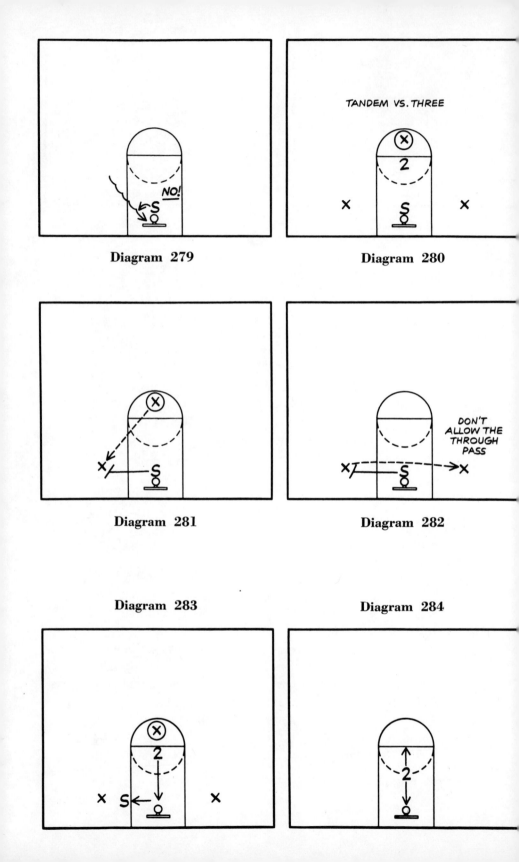

Diagram 279

Diagram 280

Diagram 281

Diagram 282

Diagram 283

Diagram 284

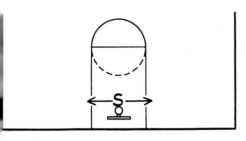

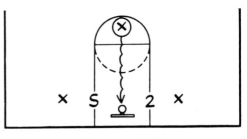

Diagram 285   Diagram 286

side and also prevents the side man from driving baseline side to the other side, Diagram 281. b) Don't allow the pass through your position to the weak side man, Diagram 282. If the ball leaves this side, it must go back to the front. c) When the ball leaves the front and goes to a side, as in Diagram 281, 2 man slides vertically back and becomes the goalie—stopping at the front of the rim, *not* under it, Diagram 283, as S goes ball-side shading the baseline side. 2 can now pick up a side man who drives top side of S. 2 can also rebound a side shot or recover forward to front x if the pass returns to the front.

S must keep one hand up as he slides sideward—this discourages the through pass. d) In summary, 2 slides *only* forward and back three steps, 2 is forward on the ball any time the ball is in front. He does not cover beyond the free throw line, Diagram 284. e) S slides *only* sideward, two steps left and/or two right, Diagram 285. He always keeps one foot inside the lane. He never covers forward and back. f) S and 2 never play side by side—it is too easy for the opponents to get to the board, especially down the middle, Diagram 286. In tandem, there are always two men, instead of the occasional "none" as in dual, in line with the ball and basket.

We practice the tandem drill often in early season.

If S and 2 can make the defense make three passes, they have succeeded. The other three defenders have surely arrived by now. If the attackers become impatient and shoot from outside, okay. We have good rebounding potential.

Pursuing

All men *sprint* back and pick up defensive assignments. If there is a time to loaf or play it easy, this *ain't* it! Collapse and pursue at sprint speed. If you need to rest, do it on offense. Arrive late and you *need not* arrive. No late arrivals in transition!

NINE

Basics of Man-to-Man

Defense

Superiority of man-to-man over the zone

Bert Taylor's comments on bread pudding are appropriate to zone defenses in the opinion of at least one coach. In paraphrase:

> . . . We love a thousand,
> we hate but one
> with a hate more hot than the hate of the gun;
> ——zone defenses!

Perhaps romanticism prevails in this attitude since one mark of the romantic is having an enemy. There is a distinct inclination to show contempt for zones herein. The zone defense is very popular and according to some evidence is becoming more popular for reasons we will mention later. There are many good zone defenses; there will no doubt always be. A specific comparison of the relative merit of each seems to be in order.

Advantages and reasons for using man-to-man

1. If you are behind in the score with time waning, man-to-man is almost a necessity. A good zone press may suffice. Maybe!

126

2. If the man-to-man *is* admittedly best and necessary at times, it is usually a meager man-to-man if played as an auxiliary or emergency defense. We feel that to be good, especially in the "clutch" when needed most, it must be played all the time. It is needed most in close or possible losing situations, therefore it should be the prime weapon.

3. Played regularly, each day in practice, it causes teammates who drill and scrimmage against it constantly to be offensively prepared and competent versus it in general. This daily offensive experience causes the most rapid and reliable skill improvement. In brief, playing against man-to-man defense consistently in practice does the most to improve *offensive* competency.

4. Similarly, daily employment of man-to-man defensive techniques and movements is the ideal way to develop *physical conditioning*. The moving, moving, always moving and the nature of these movements engenders a degree of muscular and cardio-vascular endurance in a basketball· player that can never be even closely attained by players who spend their defensive time "zoning it." For the zone player, conditioning must come otherwise.

5. Employment of a defense which constantly puts pressure on the ball and all other men creates, without question, a *pride* in players. Boys know they are playing an active game at all times, each and every second, not only on offense or only when the ball is near their position as in some zone schemes. The zone by the very nature of the name and in actuality, admits to defensing only specific areas at only certain times.

6. When man-to-man defense is employed, every offensive man is defended at all times. The offensive man is very conscious of this, he *knows* it—indeed he can hardly ignore it. The defender *knows* it, the fans *know* it, . . . yes, everybody knows it. The fans, if educated by generous experiences and example, tend to dèmand it as evidenced by the professional NBA policy. The boys who play for money seem to have grave doubts about fans paying real money to see defenses stand and wave (and slide a little) in zone defenses. Man-to-man causes and results in *ten* men playing basketball every second. It breeds action on the part of *both* the offense and defense. It simply *does more for the game*. We believe zone defenses are a real threat and a detriment to the game. We

feel they detract from the actual action potential of the great game of basketball, tend to slow it down, cause it to be more of a stand-still game than it would otherwise be. We feel that zones cause the game to be, in another way, a "stand" and shoot game and although the prime winning objective is to score, the actual shot is not as exciting (to most) as is the action which makes the shot possible or impossible.

7. My candid opinion based on the observations of many tournaments, conference champions, and national championships is that *the championships* are more frequently won by the *man-to-man teams* than by the zone teams, other things being equal. The frequency of this tendency (there have been and will be exceptions) is too obvious for me to overlook. The championships are won with man-to-man defenses. I expect to be a relative champ each season I play and I'll play the best type.

8. *Interest* is greater when man-to-man is played because:

a. man-to-man forces the offense to move.

b. encourages the offense to use intricate maneuvers.

c. each defender has an active, constant assignment and therefore his attention is usually directed to a definite interest objective.

9. Each player is challenged defensively to overpower, outdo or beat his offensive counterpart. If a defender fails, the opponent scores and everyone in the stands and on the court *knows* who failed or succeeded. In zone defense credit or liabilities are often not identifiable or possible. In man-to-man there is (usually) no doubt about responsibility, with the challenge and opportunity to be the individual winner or loser in a two-man battle.

The coach personally can accept this same challenge to use the defense which will prove him, his team and his method of defense as superior (or inferior) to his opponent.

10. There is a certain *satisfaction,* an advanced concept of joy or fun that perhaps is better appreciated and understood by the more mature player and coach which results from knowing we are playing the best (perhaps the most demanding and difficult— it *isn't* as *easy* as zone!) defense. It is furthermore rewarding and satisfying for a coach and player to realize that the previous nine (9) advantages mentioned above are forthcoming to the man-to-man defense.

11. There will be no defeats caused by the super shooter who can do nothing except stand on a spot and shoot. These shooters who otherwise cannot play can hurt a zone at long-range.

Weaknesses of man-to-man play or "alibis" for using zone!

I've used zone defenses many, many times. I've won games and championships with zones. I've been defeated by zones—both good ones and on a few occasions poor ones. I may use them again sometime. I have no quarrel with anyone who uses zone defenses. I do have an *opinion* as to why they do use them and why I used or may use them. Reasons for use of zone defense are:

1. Easy to teach compared to man-to-man. Man-to-man is not easy to teach well and efficiently.
2. Demand less time to learn.
3. Less demanding mentally.
4. Less demanding physiologically, an out-of-shape person cannot play good man-to-man for an entire game.
5. Coach perhaps does not totally know enough man-to-man principles and fundamentals to teach it effectively.
6. Probability of frequent fouling is less than in an undisciplined man-to-man. Well-coached man-to-man is not a foul prone defense.
7. Easier to transist to rebounding. Again well-coached man-to-man can achieve good rebounding.

These reasons seem feeble when compared to the advantages of playing man-to-man.

How to teach and learn man-to-man defense

Disciplined man-to-man defense is the ultimate kind. It is not easily taught or learned. It requires much energy, both mental and physical. It demands knowledge; it demands dedication. The players need to know of the actual rewards, as listed previously, which will be the pay off for this extra demand.

A boy, a team must *want* to play the best. Once having accepted man-to-man as *the* defense, it is taught and learned in three phases described as follows:

1. Head

I have found it to be a mistake to merely set out to teach man-to-man defense even though I feel capable of *explaining* and *demonstrating* it in considerable detail. In other words, after a long learning period on my own part (as a coach) I finally began to feel competent to both show and tell my boys "how it should be done" on defense. I have then, proceeded to do just this on many occasions—at the first defensive practice session I'd start delivering my best defensive lessons and working closely to a check-list, leave nothing unsaid or to be desired. There are some boys who will get it—but some will *not*. No sir—they must *first* be PRIMED.

They must first be caused, made, motivated, readied to play good man-to-man defense. The movement skills are important, yes, vitally so. The understandings, principles of when to do something, how to do it, etc. are absolutely essential, *but* first and foremost, each and every boy must be, if at all possible, caused to decide (for himself) that "I want to be first-class on defense," "I will always be an asset to our team defense," "Yes sir, coach, I *will* play the toughest defense; you can count on me," etc.

I don't know what is required to achieve this attitude in each boy, but every known and possible ethical means of motivation is necessary at one time or another. You may think all your boys want to be first-class defensive men, but too often I've heard a boy say, in restrospect to the season ended, "Coach, I could have done a little better on defense." This kind of statement is usually a most sincere and intimate admission of guilt for which the boy is willing to accept 100 percent of the blame. I've come to feel considerably responsible because I *know* by experience (and he doesn't, or didn't!), that sooner or later he will realize that he wasn't at his best.

So ... whatever it takes to make them first realize how important it is to *want* to play defense, do it—even if it means ten hours (or more) of sitting on one's rear and talking and listening at the expense of work on the floor. Some readers don't like that idea of physical idleness for mental activity's sake, and neither especially, do I. I believe, however, that most of the hard work on both the coach's and the players' part goes down the drain unless first the ideas of defense are firmly embedded in the boys' *heads*.

How? Make as clear as possible the advantages of man-to-man over the zone (or vice versa if you intend to use zone!, or both if you intend to use both!). Tell them that they will work their tails off on defense and that many times there will be no headlines, appreciation by the fans, points to show for it, etc. Tell them that they'll need courage to draw the charge fouls from opponents, they'll have black and blue rear ends—which they incidentally cannot display as proof of their defensive prowess! Tell them that in the end only *they* will know the ultimate satisfaction of playing it all the way, to the hilt, on both offense and defense.

In the following chapter there are about forty techniques, skills or whatever, that make up a (fairly) complete defensive arsenal. Tell the boys why each of these skills is important and *why;* show the team what the result of perfection is in these abilities.

Do this *before* you "learn" them how to play defense. Believe me, it is a mistake *not* to! They learn defense first in their *heads*. How to do it, why to do it a certain way, when to do certain things, in other words, the knowledge, appreciation and understandings of defense must be there first, in the *head!*

2. Feet

Most green kids visualize defense in basketball as being use of the hands. Consequently they grab, hold, get off balance, foul and in brief try to do a difficult job with hands while the rest of their bodies contribute little.

In spite of the extreme importance of the head work involved, which continues to be of prime consideration, defense next boils down to "making the feet move for you." We say that in football, "blocking is about 10 percent know and 90 percent effort." It can likewise be said in basketball that defense is about 90 percent effort after that critical 10 percent of "know" is first attained. Effort is primarily footwork. Footwork is essentially making the feet *move*. There is, of course, a lot of know-how that applies directly to footwork and the related aspects of body positioning, movement, etc. The details of footwork are covered rather completely in the next chapter. The main point here is that after the *head,* basketball defense is next learned, and played, with the *feet.*

3. *Hands*

After defense (man-to-man) has been learned in the head, then the feet, it is rather easily culminated in the use and work of the arms and hands. In fact, after the first two phases, hand-work becomes almost natural and automatic. I've never had "hand trouble" with any boy who first learned "head" and "feet" techniques.

Good use of hands becomes the pay off for man-to-man defense. Improper use of hands can scuttle the entire effort, because as every coach knows, a majority of defensive fouls tend to be arm and hand contacts.

Don't let defense be played first and/or only with hands. Show me a hand fighter on defense and I'll show you a boy who is apt to foul out *or* give up too many points.

Head, feet, hands.

"My ball and my game" or being in command while on defense

If at all possible, my boys will have developed what might be considered an unusual attitude while on defense. In summary, I want and expect this outlook from each and every man:

1. "I may be on defense, you may have the ball, but you are not going to score."
2. "You are not going to keep that ball long enough to hurt us."
3. "I like defense, but I'd rather play offense, so I'm going to play defense so intently and so effectively that I work myself right out of a (defensive) job!"
4. "You may get a few points, but they'll be accidental."
5. "We call the shots and control the ball and the game, even if you possess the ball."
6. "I believe simply that you cannot score *because* of my defensive *effort.*"

TEN

Teaching and Using

Man-to-Man

Various types of man-to-man defense

Man-to-man defense can be
played as many ways as can the zone. It may be any one or any
combination of the following: every man tight, every man loose,
one tight and four loose (sinking), full court tight, full court
loose, full court tight and loose, half or quarter court combinations, switching from loose or tight attachments, aggressive, passive, the use of body, arms, hands, etc., makes for hundreds of
variations of man-to-man defense.

In general, we play one basic defense; we use a couple of variations of it for situational effect.

Our favorite: "regular down," a five-man defense

Our defensive basketball players have only three responsibilities
while on defense: 1) their own men, 2) everyone else's man, if
necessary, 3) the ball.

We attempt to achieve this task by the following plan. The
man on the ball plays very aggressively and closely. The men
playing distant from the ball play relatively loose and the men
closer to the ball play relatively tight. Thus every man is some-

what able to support the ball man if his aggressiveness results in error. This plan is generally called a "sinking defense."

Where *to* Stand *and Why* (*Alignment*)

If the offensive team should assume floor positions as in Diagram 287, the defensive alignment would appear as shown.

Number 1 would play tight as shown. Number 2 is "one pass removed" from the ball, so his alignment rule is: one step back toward the basket and one step over (toward) the ball. Notice that 2 is thereby loose and ball-side. In case the pass is made to his man, he is in interception position, yet he is also able to: a) recover and stay between his man and the basket should his man get the ball and, b) help 1 by stopping an attempted drive to the right side of 1.

Number 4 is also "one pass removed" and his rule is the same as the rule for 2.

Number 3 is "two passes removed," his alignment rule is: two steps toward the basket and two steps toward the ball. This rule enables 4 to police the hoop in case the primary defense of 1 should fail and should the secondary defense of 2 and 4 fail. In effect, 4 is the third line of resistance, yet he is able to maintain pressure on his man who cannot get the ball quickly.

For purposes of illustration, 5, the post man, plays an individual game if there is an offensive pivot man. We will not discuss his coverage until later.

In summary, the man on the ball is tight; the farther from the basket and/or the ball, the less tight is the defensive attachment.

After players understand where to *align,* introduce next where to *face* and look.

Where *to* Face *and* Look (*Positioning*)

Number 1 faces the man with the ball and of course can see both man and the ball. What about 2, does he watch ball *or* the man? The answer is *both* and he is able to do so by using the following guidelines for men who are defending "empty men" or men without the ball.

"Empty man positioning rule"

Draw an imaginary dotted line on the deck connecting the man you are covering and the basketball, Diagram 288. Point

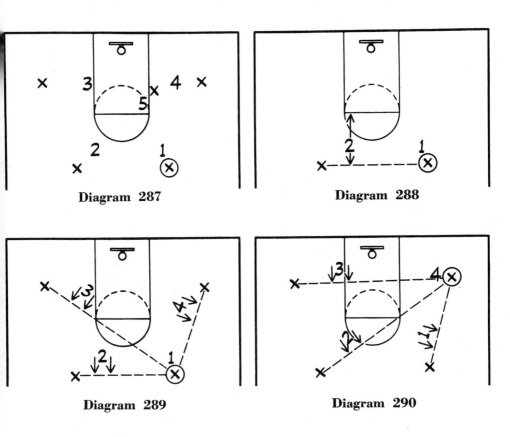

Diagram 287

Diagram 288

Diagram 289

Diagram 290

both feet perpendicular to this dotted line. Now, depending on your peripheral vision, move closer to this line or farther from it until, with your face also perpendicular to this line (Don't turn the head right or left) you can see both the ball and *your* own man. The distance you play from the imaginary dotted line is determined by a) your own peripheral vision, b) your own reaction time and speed, c) speed of your opponent.

The distance you play from your *man* (ball-side distance) is determined by the distance *he* is from the ball. The nearer he is to the ball, the less your drift away from him and the less you play the ball-side.

Diagram 289 shows how 3 would position himself relative to *his* dotted line and how 4 would adjust.

Should the ball be passed or moved to *any* other spot on the floor, all the dotted lines would change and hence *all* empty defensive men would have to move and readjust their positioning! In Diagram 290, notice how all men, 1, 2, and 3 are now oriented differently as the ball moved from the right guard position down to the corner. Had the right guard dribbled only one or two steps

135

in any direction, all other defensive men would of necessity, change their position.

How *to* Stand (*Stance, Balance*)

The man on the ball assumes a stance that is comfortable to him. We like this to resemble a modified boxer's stance with one foot forward and one to the rear. The defensive man is crouched as *low as possible!* His head is up and his tail is low. We tell him to keep the eyes about the same height as the opponent's nipples, or "eyeballs to nipples." Bend the knees and get the tail down toward the heels. Now get the tail 6 inches lower. Always keep the tail lower than you are inclined to. The rear heel tends to rise off the deck as the knees bend. Do not allow this to occur. Rear heel must stay on the floor. Do not allow the upper body to lean too far forward and thus transfer the weight to the front foot. Weight must be about 80 percent on the rear foot because the critical movements you will be making will be rearward and you cannot move backwards if your weight is forward, and your weight *will* be forward *if* the rear heel is up. The only weight you need forward is one or two pounds on the basketball. You can block passes, shots, etc. with only a few ounces of hand pressure.

The distance from the offensive man should be about 1 1/2 steps. You should be able to touch the offensive man's chest between his nipples if you take a short forward stride with your front foot.

These suggestions enable the defender to move with his man yet exert pressure on the ball. We want our defensive man to play as far away from the offensive man as possible and at the same time *appear* (to the offensive man) to be as close as possible!

The defender should normally position himself slightly (about six inches) to the strong side of the opponent. If the opponent is right-handed, our defensive man straddles the right leg of the opponent, staying of course, 1 1/2 strides away. If, however, he is apt to drive left—even though he be right-handed—such as a left corner man the defender may overplay to the left to protect the baseline, or for some other reasons. Normally we expect front line defenders to overplay slightly to the middle (center) of the court and force drivers to the sidelines. Once the ball is on the sideline we attempt to force it back to the middle by overplaying on the sideline side. At the baseline we always play baseline side and try to force the offender topside.

Pointing the Ball

One (not two) hands of the defender should always be pointing at the basketball as it is held, dribbled, faked, shot or passed. The offensive man must always be conscious of the fact that a defensive hand is near, intent on trouble. Should the offensive man become careless, this "pointing" hand will have the ball deflected, stolen, blocked. *Always* keep a hand "in there" even though you may fail by three feet to reach the ball. Do not allow this to be a locked elbow, stiff arm reach. Keep it firm but not rigid—keep it always "in there." This gesture also informs your defensive mates that "he belongs to me!"

How *to* Move

We first want the defensive man to know where to align, where to face, how to stand and only after these concepts have been fairly well understood do we attempt to teach him movement as part of the defensive scheme.

The defender must, first and foremost, *keep his feet under him!* He must make his feet move. Each time the opponent moves the defender must move (one exception to be covered later); the feet must move briskly and preferably in short, hard and violent steps. The feet should be on the floor most of the time; they should not be in transit (floating from place to place in the air!) except minimally. If one thing is important above all others in defensive efficiency, it is how often, briskly and violently the feet move! The shorter the steps, the better. If the defender waits so long that he needs to take a long step, he is already at a disadvantage.

The defender's first move should begin from a staggered stance (one of his feet will be forward). Some coaches teach players to keep "outside foot forward," or "keep your foot forward to his strong side." There are special occasions in which we also do this, but usually the forward foot is the choice of the individual defender based on natural tendency and comfort.

If the offensive man with the ball moves forward, right or left, the first defensive reaction is always one and the same: step back with the front foot into a parallel stance. This means, of course, changing from a staggered to a parallel stance. The tendency is to step back with the back foot. This results in an exaggerated awkward spread-eagle position. Do not permit the rear foot to move until after the front foot has moved back.

After the slide to the parallel stance, the defender can go right or left by shuffle steps. The shuffle step is open with the right foot (to go right) and bring the left foot up to it. It can be described as lead with the front foot and close with the trailing foot: step—close, step—close, etc. To go left, it would be lead left foot, close right foot, etc. If the offensive man continues to go forward, that is, near and past the defender, the defender does *not* back-pedal. He makes a quarter turn and shuffles so long as he can keep pace with the driver or cutter. If he lags behind in this foot race, then and only then does he stop the shuffle steps and runs, one leg alternating ahead of the other.

In general, always shuffle step and never cross over step (run) unless you have been left out of position. In this case, run to proper location and resume shuffling.

The one exception to assuming a parallel stance noted previously is if the opponent moves backward. In this case the defender does not move into a parallel stance, but should stand still and not adjust or shuffle forward.

Again, we repeat, first move into a parallel stance regardless of which way your opponent goes and regardless of which foot is your forward foot. This eliminates 90 percent of the confusion about which foot should move first and which foot belongs where.

Where to Travel in Moving

Most of the problems of defense arise as the defensive man is on the move. It is one thing to play defense on a standing opponent; it is something else to properly defend a driver or a cutter!

The first thing a defender should do as he starts to move about the floor is to glance quickly at his intended travel route and observe the congestion which he might encounter. "Do not fly blind on a basketball floor while on defense." The best way to avoid screening problems is to avoid the screens rather than to escape them after becoming entangled.

The defender should attempt always to stay one-half stride in advance of the cutter or driver. Should he reverse, the defender can regain position in time. Other considerations for movement appear in the following paragraphs.

AVOIDING SCREENS

We don't expect to be screened. In order that we will not be screened, several techniques must be learned. The first lesson is to recognize that there are several kinds of screens, some more dangerous than others. One such screen is the paired screen as shown in Diagram 291. If the man with the ball, defended by 2, starts toward the other offenser and 1, 2 must get there *first* and of course see both his teammate and the other opponent, either of whom can be effective as a screener on him. In general, this side screen is the easiest to work against and we initiate defenders by working them first against the paired-side screen.

The most difficult screen is the rear screen, Diagram 292. Defender 2 must listen for footsteps behind him, listen for heavy breathing of the screener, listen for warnings by teammates (we always warn teammates of rear screens only).

We tell defenders that there are three places to go in avoiding screens particularly the paired-side screen, over, through, and under, Diagram 293.

When, Why, and How to Go Over Screens

The defender should go *over* (the top of) screens whenever:
1. the screen is approximately 18 feet or nearer the basket, or
2. the opponent is good enough in shooting to be a rather sure bet to score even if in excess of that distance. In order to go "over," the defender must of course *get* there *first!*

When, Why, and How to Go Through Screens

The defender goes *through* the paired screen whenever:
1. he is at the middle distance range where a shot by his opponent from over the screen is unlikely although possible, or
2. any time the defender is uncertain as to whether he should go under, through or over. "If in doubt, always go through."

Diagram 291	Diagram 292

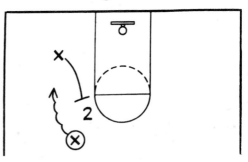

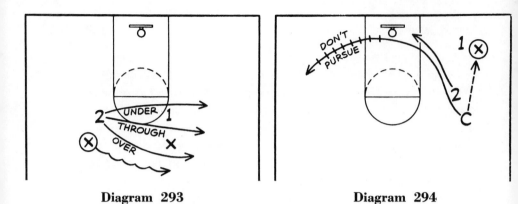

Diagram 293   **Diagram 294**

When, Why and How to go Behind (Under) Screens

The defensive man goes behind all such screens whenever:
1. the range is too great for the shot to be a threat, and
2. any time the opponent is not considered a shooting threat even at close range.

Feeling and Fighting the Screen Effect

The skills of avoiding and escaping screens are: 1) Know the screen is there. One of the most pitiful sights known to me is to see a defensive player collide with a screen because he was unaware! Look and listen and feel for it. The lead arm should always be groping for obstacles whenever the defender moves backward or to a blind side. 2) If there is a screen, arrive there *before* the offensive man; thus you can with a higher probability escape or avoid it before your opponent arrives. 3) If you must fight the screen pressure, employ any or all of these techniques: If you are going "over" the screen, a) "throw through" the narrow space between the screener and the driver by going through sideways, draw in your abdomen, stretch tall and throw vigorously your arms through first; this will tend to pull your body through the narrow space. b) If you are going through the screen expect your teammate to grab your hips at the beltline and pull or force you through the congestion. c) If you don't get physical force help from your buddy, you may profit by elbowing or shoving *him* out of the way. He, of course, should not be in a position which will retard your progress. d) If you are going under the screen, you can occasionally profit by grasping your buddy at the waist and using him for a fulcrum to change directions in case your opponent reverses, etc.

140

DEFENSING THE CUTTER

We define a cutter as an offensive man without the ball who is moving rapidly toward a screen and/or the goal. There are a couple of rules which govern defensing cutters. 1) Always go ball side of cutters; never allow a cutter to feed a teammate and then get between you and the ball, for a possible return feed. 2) Keep your hands high and moving as the cutter approaches the goal. This restricts his potential as a late pass recipient. 3) *Never* pursue cutters away from the goal because they will not be fed, or they will not be dangerous if fed, Diagram 294; they will return if they want to play, so slack off and only partially (very loosely) follow them. 4) Never pursue cutters away from the ball, except loosely, for the same reasons described in 3 above, Diagram 295.

DEFENSING THE DRIVER

Drivers are cutters in possession of the ball. In addition to the guidelines for defensing cutters, which apply generally also to drivers, we try to teach defensive men to 1) Stay away from drivers at least a forearm's distance. This gives sufficient space to use the arms and hands and not foul. We believe that if an opponent ever gets closer than a forearm's distance to us, the advantages are in favor of the offense. 2) Stay low and keep the hands withdrawn and the elbows close to the belt. If you are running side by side with the driver, *don't fight* him *enroute.* Sprint and get ahead of him, set up camp and then take him to task. If you reach across the body of drivers, you are apt to foul, and you are also apt to be drawn off balance and hence put at a greater disadvantage. 3) Other aspects of defensing drivers are covered under the following topics.

HELP VERSUS SWITCHING

In reviewing our basic defense "Regular Down," the one man who is defensing the ball man is tight and quite aggressive. The remaining four defenders are one, two, or three steps off their respective men depending on the proximity of these offensers to the basketball. Should the ball man defender lose defensive control of his opponent, the other four men can offer some aid. Thus every player assists the ball defender.

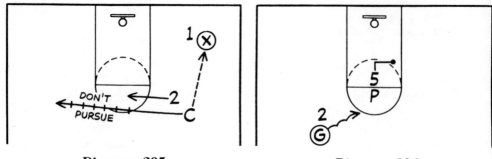

Diagram 295   Diagram 296

We do not switch in our Regular Down game. I sincerely believe that a good switch game is the most effective game in basketball. I also believe it is impractical and impossible to teach perfectly. I've never seen a foolproof switch game. So—we do not switch on defense. I'll hasten to admit that we do switch as a special situational "gimmick" which is not part of Regular Down, our basic defense. We do "Help," and here is what is meant by "Help."

Help is a temporary or false switch. It appears to be a switch, but actually is not. It can be described as: "Moving back one step and over a step" into the traffic route of a driver (or cutter). It is employed most by post men and forwards, but everyone uses the Help maneuver. It is fairly easy to learn.

In Diagram 296, G with the ball gains a half step advantage and starts over P in an attempt to rub 2 off on P and/or 5. If 5 will "help," the drive threat of G can be eliminated. In order to do this, 5 steps *back* one step. This accomplishes the following: 1) Gives 2 room to pass behind P and take a short cut route to intercept G, Diagram 297. 2) In case P decides to roll to the basket, 5 can see this action and is still essentially in good position between P and the hoop.

Five then steps *over* one step and solidly sets up directly in the path of the driver, G. Thus, G must: 1) charge 5, or 2) reverse back into 2 pursuing, Diagram 298, or 3) widen his route, which drives him away from the basket area and allows 2 to regain defensive pressure on G, Diagram 299.

The Help lasts only a brief time. In effect 5 is telling 2: "If you stumble or lose your balance, I'll delay your opponent briefly. I'll keep him away from a direct route to the hoop only long enough for you to scramble and re-attach to him, *then* I again get my own man." Five is primarily interested in P, but will handle both jobs at once if it means preventing a score. Perhaps G will

142

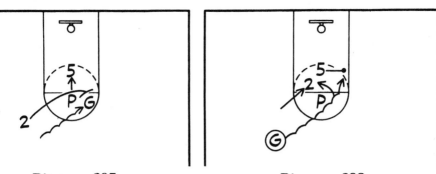

Diagram 297   **Diagram 298**

score anyway—later! It is to the advantage of the defense to *delay* the scoring even if only for one second. If this situation occurs ten times a game, ten seconds of time has been salvaged and a team might do considerable in ten precious seconds!

In summary, Help is a temporary false switch. It is used by any and all defensive men who see a teammate in front or to the side of them who gets "into trouble." It is not called or requested by the man in trouble. The rear-most defender can see the danger develop and our rule which determines whether or not we Help is this: If you can delay or stop a driver by Helping, and if he will pass within one (long) step of you, always Help. The front or original defender is reminded that *he* continues to be responsible for his man and we demand that no player "depend" on Help.

As new players become adept at Helping, we extend the action to one step back and two steps over and can often be effective on any driver within two long steps (12 feet) of our position.

Switching is a different technique. We practice jump switching and use it primarily to bolster our offensive game in practice. We use jump switches in special situations (presses, auxiliary defenses such as 94, Regular Up, etc. which are described later) but not normally in Regular Down.

The main difference in the jump switch ("jump" means the rear man jumps into the switch rather than stepping into it) and switch is that rear man (5) jumps *forward* a step (instead of *back* as in Help), Diagram 300.

In regard to switching, we insist on these few rules. 1) The *rear* man (5 in this case) will decide if there will be a switch because only he can see the total action. Two cannot call for it because he cannot see his man and 5 and P. Only the rear man decides. The front man may "call" for it, but it is merely a request, not a command, which 5 may or may not accept. 2) It must

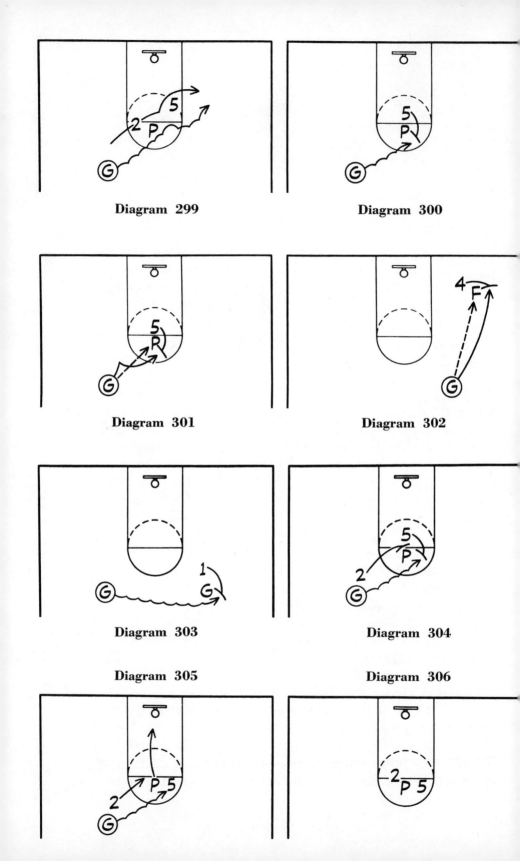

Diagram 299

Diagram 300

Diagram 301

Diagram 302

Diagram 303

Diagram 304

Diagram 305

Diagram 306

be *early*. Five must "be there" before G arrives so that if contact ensues, G has charged. I want no block fouls on 5 because of the inability of 2 to handle his man; 5 must be there *before* G passes beyond P. 3) It must be *aggressive:* 5 must "mean business." There must be no doubt that 5 welcomes all the trouble G can offer. No passive or half-hearted switches. 4) If the offensive maneuver is a feed-and-cut, with a return hand-off to the cutter, as in a post split, Diagram 301, 5 must jump switch *before* the ball bounces.

As do many teams, we jump switch on post splits, vertical moves, Diagram 302 and all cross or lateral moves, Diagram 303.

The reason for the jump is that the switcher (rear man) can get into position *quicker* by jumping from both feet and landing on both feet. He is also, and this is very important, *legally* entitled to the position the instant both feet touch the deck—he has "established" himself according to the rules.

The play of the front man, the man originally responsible for the driver or cutter also is different for switching than in Help. Whereas in Help the front man pursues his original opponent and reattaches to him—diagrams 297, 298, and 299—in the switch he must assume coverage on the other opponent, the one originally defended by the jump switcher. In Diagram 304, 2 rushes to cover P. He must do this very quickly and without delay, otherwise P may roll to the basket, Diagram 305. Two should lag slightly to his approach side of P as 5 is established slightly on the opposite side, Diagram 306. This serves two purposes: 1) It enables both 2 and 5 to exert some double-team pressure on P if he gets or keeps the ball, and 2) If G reverses and comes back in order to escape 5's jump switch, 2 can immediately jump switch on G and consequently 5 can recover to P, Diagram 307. It is good practice to jump switch and re-switch. It teaches both defenders to be alert to the roll by the screener and the reverse by the cutter.

How do boys know whether it will be a Help or a Switch? 1) It will always be Help unless, 2) Coach has indicated previously that switching will be employed. If this be the case, the *rear* man will decide if and when to switch. The *front* man will know by *seeing* the action develop. If Help is forthcoming, then: 3) rear man will step *back* and over; this is front man's cue to fight through the screen and re-attach to the cutter, ignore the screener. If switch is forthcoming, the rear man will be *up* (not back) and the front man will instantly become concerned for the *screener,* Diagrams 308 and 309.

The rear man determines it. The front man is taught to recognize it. I don't believe in pre-determining switches since the rear man may not be able to carry out the switch because the screener may go early, or some other reason.

COLLAPSING

Should the front defender, 2 for example, falter and allow G to penetrate the defense, all other men try to Help. We exert pressure from all sides, which we call molesting (described later). The front man originally on the ball does not relax and relinquish his coverage; instead he pursues at sprint speed and harasses from the rear, tries to regain a lead position and in brief, goes at the basket one degree or more vigorously than does the offensive man.

POST PLAY DEFENSE

We teach *all* team members to play offensive post (wheeling, drag, etc.) and likewise we teach defensive post play to all men. Each and every man will find himself defending men in the pivot area at various times during each game and season.

The first lesson for defensive post play is recognition of the three types of posts: low, medium, and high.

Low Posts

Any offensive man in the vicinity of the board (within two long steps of the basket) is considered as a Low Post. He may be on the baseline, in the lane, on either side of the lane, stationary or moving, Diagram 310.

The basic rule for defensing low posts: "Play on *top* of a low post."

The defender plays "on top" by facing the ball either completely or partially. He *never* faces the low post man at the expense of losing sight of the ball.

Should the offensive low post play back under the board on one side with the ball in front on the opposite side, as in Diagram 311, defender 5 would face the ball, position himself about three feet away from the low post, keep eyes alert for the low post moving quickly right or left past the defender to the ball. If the low post cannot be seen with peripheral vision and *without* turning the head, defensive man *knows* (even though he cannot see)

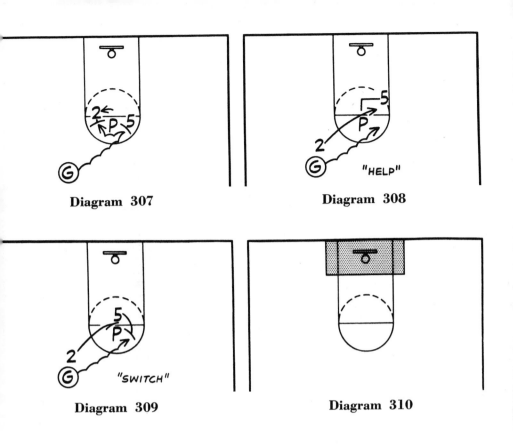

Diagram 307

Diagram 308

"HELP"

Diagram 309

"SWITCH"

Diagram 310

where the low post man is—directly behind the defender. So long as he remains there he is well-defended. Should the defender turn his head, the low post will probably dart around the defender on the opposite side of the turned head and get "above" or ball-side, receive the ball and score easily.

In summary, use the ears, eyes, feelers (both hands down and back slightly) and don't look for him by turning the head. Stay on top of him.

Medium Posts, In and Out of Line

Any offensive man near or in the lane within two to three steps of the basket is a Medium Post. The basic rule for defensing is: "Play *beside* medium posts."

There are a few complications that need attention as one attempts to fulfill this rule.

If the medium post is set "in line" (on a line drawn from the ball to the basket), Diagram 312, the defender must choose which side of the post to play. If the post is right-handed he will usually be most adept at going counterclockwise or to his right (after facing the basket). The defender should play on the lane side in

147

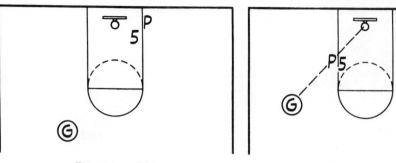

| Diagram 311 | Diagram 312 |

these cases. Should a medium post man be a good baseline driver, he might be best defended on the corner side. We determine as soon as possible in a game which side to play medium posts, lane or corner side.

If the medium post is set "out of line," Diagram 313, the defense always plays ball-side.

If the post man is originally out of line, then moves to the opposite side, Diagram 313, the defender must change sides about the time that the post man crosses the "line." The changing should be "over" the post man rather than behind him. During this brief moment, he is considered a low post. Medium post defenders should face sideways to the post men and attempt to keep the ball from reaching the post, but not so aggressively as to cause fouls.

High Post Play

Any offenser at or near the free throw line is considered a High Post. Always play *under* the high posts.

Feeders, Shooters, Screeners, Decoys

A high post should be considered as one of these four types. As soon as the high post is categorized accordingly, we apply the following coverage considerations.

A feeder will be played no closer than three feet to the rear. The defender will be loose so that he can Help on cutters and drivers and so that teammates can go through on the movements.

A shooter will be played about 1 1/2 feet or forearm distance. We will not get closer and certainly not engage (contact) him *until he turns* around because he will not score until he turns. He is not dangerous so long as he faces out!

A screener is played as a feeder (loose). The defensive post men should never allow the pivot men to feel them constantly

148

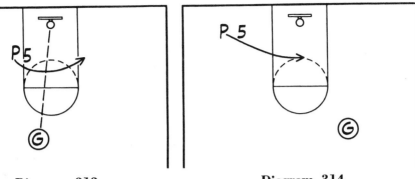

Diagram 313   **Diagram 314**

or otherwise always realize where they are. If a good pivot man can keep tab on the defense he has an advantage. Defensive post men must move around and thwart this knowledge.

Decoys or post men who essentially do none of the three previously mentioned tasks well can be partially ignored and the post defender can be useful if he plays a one-man zone in the lane. We like to give a new post man a chance, early in the game, to prove he is not a decoy.

Flash Posts

Every team member must master defensing the flash post. Each year several opponents confront us with a flash post offense as their basic attack. In Diagram 314, if P gets to or beyond the lane before 5 does, G will feed him and because P is on the move, 5 will not have much chance to stop P's roll to the board or his quick shot. We do this the first practices as a defensive reaction drill. Five simply must arrive ball-side *before* he arrives at the lane and continue to stay ball-side! He must remember to: 1) always give *some* attention to the man, never turn to watch the ball because in one brief instant, P is gone (you've been flashed!). 2) keep knees bent and be ready to start to the ball the instant P makes a move. If 5 allows P to get under way first, P will flash and 5 will bring up the rear!

Everyone must *master* this defensive skill. Be *ready* and *stay* ball-side!

Baseline Protection

Hell hath no fury like that which erupts from our bench when a defender allows an opponent to drive past him near the baseline, Diagram 315. Each and every defensive man knows that whenever his man approaches the baseline or initially positions himself near it, the defender must become baseline conscious. If the driver goes baseline he will probably score or the defender will probably foul or both!

There is no Help on the baseline side. Force him to the front or topside; there are four teammates there who might help. In order to protect the baseline, we: 1) overplay by positioning 8 to 14 inches to that side, or 2) seal off the initial first step of the offensive man by extending the baseline side foot of the defender forward to a point slightly beyond the position of the offender, or 3) both.

Baseline, baseline, baseline! Never on the baseline side!

Molesting

If an offensive maneuver penetrates the periphery of our Regular Down defense, I expect ten pairs of hands to threaten him from all sides. We plan to gain control of the ball at least four times per game in this way and in addition cause two or more jump ball situations. We often refer to this as our Hornets' Nest. Come on in!

Loose Balls

One of the four things I always tell the five starters as they leave the huddle to start the game is "All loose balls belong to us." A loose ball is a loose ball for no longer than 1/2 second. By the end of that time, let's own it. A few bruises may ensue, but loose ball retrievers are down-on-the-deck players. Go get it. NOW.

DEFENSIVE ADJUSTMENTS AS THE SHOT IS TAKEN

As the opponents shoot the ball, the defense has one of two possible reactions. Either we assume man-to-man contact with our respective men or set a five-man defensive rebounding cup. We usually set the cup whenever we use Regular Down. Man-to-man coverage will be discussed in the next chapter under Regular Down defense.

FIVE-MAN CUP AND ITS VALUE

The instant the shot leaves the shooter's hand, we abandon our man-to-man concept and go for the ball by anticipating the spots to which we expect the ball to fall. The basic rebound triangle is identical to that of the 3 1/2 offensive cup described earlier; the top two spots at the free throw line differ, Diagram 316.

Inasmuch as half of all missed shots will rebound about half as far as they are shot, many fall 15 feet or farther out. We want a man at each side of the circle. Don't let them get closer, they'll want to! Get these long rebounds and go score. Miss these long rebounds and give up points!

From this five-man cup the defense is easily changed to offense.

Individual rebounding techniques

Rebounding is a crucial phase of basketball and I feel a need to know more about it. In addition to encouraging leg strength by weight training and resistive exercises, I stress three general coaching considerations for rebounding beyond the team plan, the five-man cup.

1. Being there. Don't stand on one spot and try to reach elsewhere to rebound. You'll foul, get off balance and the distance is too great. If you want the ball first *go there, then* rebound (go up!).

2. Boxing. At the shot, give a bit of attention to your opponent, then direct your attention to the ball, but *always* remain conscious of your man. Don't let his *feet* get inside your feet; you accomplish this by imagining you had a lance attached to your rear above your tail bone. Impale him gently on this imaginary lance and *keep* him there.

3. Jump timing. For most men, do not leave the floor until the ball descends below rim height. This point is the best help of all to most boys.

General rules for defense

In addition to the ideas mentioned previously, we believe that

Diagram 315   Diagram 316

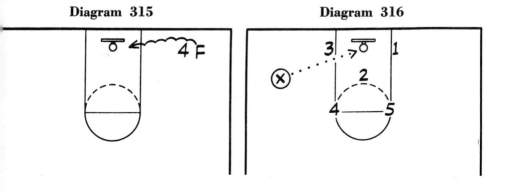

some very thorough treatment is necessary regarding jumping. Jumping rule: "Never jump while on defense" (playing the man with the ball) unless 1) He leaves the floor (jump) first, or 2) You *know* for sure he is going to jump; 95 percent of the time you do not know and cannot know!

Some teams, especially in high school, base most of their offense upon faking the jump shot to get the defender to jump, then drive past him. Modern trends show most defenses jumping. Not mine!

Defensing Jump Shooters

Although we have no foolproof jump shot defense we teach the following points which are somewhat effective: 1) Don't let him bring the ball up in a straight and direct line. Keep a hand near his chin so that he must swing the ball sideward to get it up to shooting position. This tends to a) delay the shot and disrupt the timing, and b) gets the shooter slightly off balance and affects accuracy. 2) Don't let him bounce the ball if he wants to or needs to. Most jump shooters are better if they can dribble first. 3) Don't let him get to his favorite spot on the floor. Many boys are effective only from spots. 4) Don't let him go the way he wants to go; force him the wrong way by overplay. 5) Keep hands in vertical tandem. Keep one hand at eye level to distract his aim and the other hand directly below it at chin or chest level to prevent the ball coming up. The top hand should oscillate slightly sideward; the lower hand should remain rather motionless. This positioning of hands is awkward at first, but somewhat effective.

Defensing Lay-Up Men

If a driver escapes our best defense and becomes a lay-up shooter, our philosophy is that we've done *about* all we can and the first thing we are *not* going to do is foul him. We do, however, attempt to convince him we may assassinate him by verbal noise, gestures, etc. We try to deflect the shot or dribble, but do not invite the official to suspect contact. If you foul your man after he has earned a lay-up, you've added insult to the already severe injury.

Defensing the Free Throw Shooter

Just a few minutes of attention need be given to applying defensive pressure to an opposing free throw shooter after his attempt ends. One man must be near the circle who can step in and prevent 1) the long rebound back to the free throw shooter after the free throw, and 2) the feed out to this player following a rebound by a team mate.

DEFENSING DOUBLE AND TRIPLE SCREENS

The best solution to double and/or triple screens is to switch. We always switch on these deals but do so only on a request call by the defender whose man escapes coverage and uses the screen. Who switches?—the man (any man) who is nearest the free man. Very simple to apply, but be sure and condition all men to it before it occurs in a game. The nearest man to the free opponent picks him up; the *next* nearest man may need to switch to adjust to this move. In fact, all five men may need to switch in succession to compensate for the first switch in case the original defender cannot assume coverage for the first switcher.

Double and Triple screens are very effective. One consolation is that they are somewhat slow in developing and the defense should destroy or prevent their development, rather than fight the after-effects.

Conducting practice sessions to teach defense

All defensive skills are learned in the one-on-one, two-on-two, three-on-three or five-on-five drills that are used to teach offense, covered in Chapter 7. We use only one defensive drill in addition to defensing those offensive drills. This single defensive drill is what we call "shadow defense." We use it at the end of practice and go for three to five minutes uninterrupted. All men assume a defensive stance anywhere on the floor at least 6 feet from the nearest teammate. The coach uses hand signals and a whistle to cause movements forward, sideward, backward, diagonally and to stop but maintain a defensive "ready" position. We do not allow knees to straighten or hands to touch thighs (if so, we start anew!). In addition to these directional slides (always shuffling) we drill on the half pivot to the rear from a lateral shuffle. For example, as we face south and move left (east) we call "turn" and each man plants his lead (left foot) swing, the right foot to the rear a full one-half turn so that the body is facing the opposite direction (north); his right foot now becomes his lead foot as he continues to shuffle east without lateral interruption. One more "turn" call going east and he is again facing south. Always use a rear pivot as it creates better coordination.

After three to five minutes of shadow defense fatigue is severe. We loosen up with a few high speed lay-ups and hit the shower. This drill creates endurance and defensive ability.

Summary of defense

There are hundreds of defensive skills, yet three clues to defensive effectiveness stand out. If a man keeps his tail down *low* and makes his feet move and work, and always keeps a hand at or on the ball, he is playing defense.

ELEVEN

"Regular Up," an
Auxiliary Variation

How Regular Up differs from Regular Down

Whereas Regular Down features one man playing very aggressively on the ball with the other four men in a sink or "down," and in a low or "down" stance, Regular Up means to us that all five men are "up" close to their man in an aggressive, tight position. In Regular Down, everyone offers aid to the ball defender, if necessary. In Regular Up, each man gives most of his attention to his own man and each is "on his own." In Regular Down the interior of the defense is tough and well protected; in Regular Up the emphasis and strength is on the periphery. In Regular Down the penetration is difficult and the offense must score from outside (we hope), whereas the scoring, if it occurs in Regular Up will probably come after penetration because of the outside pressure.

Advantages and uses

Regular Up is somewhat a pressure defense. It is difficult to play properly at any time; it is a taxing game for the defender. It is the ultimate defense because of simplicity of assignment, merely handle your own man alone and without any help. There is very

155

little Helping in this defense and considerable switching. If we plan to use switches, most of the time it will be from the Regular Up game.

Regular Down and Regular Up are compared in Diagrams 317 and 318. We have two main thoughts in mind as we play Regular Up. 1) *Overplay.* All men play ball-side of their opponents and try to keep the man from getting possession. This puts them in interception position should the feed attempt be made. Good continuous footwork keeps them in position to intercept. If the offensive man moves—as he must—we "dog" him constantly and attempt to tire him, harass him into fatigue, rush him into errors, or discourage him into becoming a "stand-still" player. 2) The effect this variation gives our basic defense (Regular Down). It appears to the casual observer to be the same defense but the effect is vastly different. We are able to change the pace of the game by this variation.

When to use in practice

After Regular Down, the basic defense, has been fairly well instilled in early pre-season practice, we tend to use Regular Up much more in practice because it is more demanding physically, it keeps players active and in shape, it improves their individual defense because they cannot rely on much aid from teammates, and it forces the offensive men to be more effective and skilled.

When we scrimmage, we usually employ Regular Up because of these reasons.

When to use in games

As we implied earlier, this "Up" variation is demanding physically if played over a long period. We prefer to use "Down" in games, and normally will play Regular Up only if the basic defense fails. If we get behind or the basic defense is faltering, our first variation is to go Up.

We also find that in about the last 1/3 of each season, Regular Up is almost a necessity. Why, I cannot say, except that the offense seems to have caught up with defense by then. I can only report that over the past many seasons we have had to rely on Regular Up as the season comes to an end.

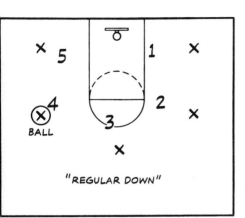

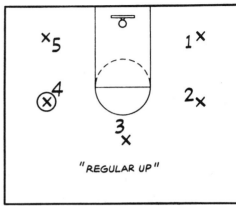

Diagram 317   Diagram 318

The details of these differences are more completely covered in the following chapter on pressure defense.

The effectiveness of any defense depends upon, first, the quality of execution by the defensive players and, second, the action or quality of attack by the offense. Some offenses exert considerable strain on the basic Regular Down game. It seems wise for a team to have an effective variation which is compatible to the basic defense but which will give a different "look" to the opponents. Regular Up does not interfere with the learnings in Regular Down, yet it often prevents offensive success.

Regular Up is more susceptible to screens than is the Down game because the defender is close and giving so much of his attention to the man that screeners are noticed less.

TWELVE

Pressure Man-to-Man

Defense

94, the full court press

The most difficult of all man-to-man defenses to play effectively is the full court pressure game. Can five men defend (50 x 94) 4700 square feet of area? If so, it will be only with the finest execution of sound principles. It is a difficult job and versus some teams an impossible one. On the other hand, if you play to "win them all" the obvious conclusion is that there will be times when defense must cover 4700 square feet. The zone press may be the answer, then again, you may win one only by doing it the hard way, or "94" ("94" because we play it for 94 linear feet of floor, from baseline to baseline).

Used regularly in practice, 94 develops all-around defensive skills (e.g. endurance, concentration, high speed footwork, etc.), that improve the other aspects of the game.

Advantages of pressure beyond normal shooting range

First of all, 94 will cause all but the best coached and/or highly skilled teams to change their offensive game. If a team is a pattern team or a team that prefers to "set up" in formation before attacking, a good press allows no laxity for this. Some teams are well-drilled versus the zone press and by moving the ball properly with two or three better players, can defeat the zone. If teams of this sort face pressure to a man, constantly, perhaps there is no outlet opportunity which allows any relaxation or respite. A team that has mastered man-to-man play as their basic defense can present a fairly efficient full court man-to-man press with but a few additional new learnings. Ideally, the full court press is essentially the same as the basic defense. We believe it should be played often in practice, especially in early season, because: 1) the basic defense (Regular Down) benefits, 2) the press game is perfected, and 3) the press advance is polished. Only the first of these advantages accrues if the basic defense is most used in practice.

We prefer to play 94 only in short spurts in games. I usually, at a time out, ask "Do we have enough steam to 94 it for two minutes, full throttle and no let up?" The answer is usually "Certainly, coach!" as I repeat the question to each and every man. They then do it. Ask for five minutes and they'll sincerely try it but the result will be less than perfect and then the confidence held by the players in 94 will be less the next time it's applied. Our favorite technique is alternate a full team each five minutes—when I have ten worthies!

Additional advantages are: 1) surprise effect to opponents, 2) rejuvenation of our own spirit as we step up the aggression tempo of our defense, and 3) one quick basket gained as a result of the opponents' offensive error, caused by defensive harassment is very apt to lead to another, and another. The second and subsequent baskets come easier because the embarrassment caused by the first one contributes to tension and further inefficiency on the part of the offense ... usually!

Weaknesses, disadvantages, and liabilities

1) If one man fails to remember to apply pressure on his man immediately as defense begins, the entire effort fails. The most common mistake is one man forgetting just for an instant. His man gets free, gets the ball and away they go. 2) If a team is not in perfect endurance condition, the full court man-to-man press is rarely good. 3) If there are not five capable substitutes available 94 is of limited value. 4) Once an offensive team starts penetration to the goal, 94 cannot exert adequate defense to reliably stop scoring. 5) One very good floor man can hurt this

defense. 6) A tall team that can move the ball well is trouble for 94.

Overplay and rules to govern its teaching and learning

In Regular Up we usually overplay and often double-team. In 94 we *always* do both. Overplay is the basic essential of the good man-to-man press. The basic overplay rule is: As the man on the ball plays over-aggressively, the next two nearest men play ball-side (interception) position in anticipation of the outlet feed. The offense then has two choices, both of which are not conducive to their success. They may attempt to feed and risk interception or they may withhold the outlet feed and risk a tie-up, a five second count or the resultant slow-down of their normal rhythm or game tempo.

Overplay drill, ball forcing, and ball-side

We teach overplay in two drills. The first and basic drill is a two-on-two plan, Diagram 319. Both defensive men have a definite learning assignment. 1) The ball defender learns to overplay *away* from the most probable outlet side. We want 1 to give X only one possible side to go or feed. This simplifies 1's job and also 2's job. X cannot go to his left, he must go right to 2's interception or double team. Two, the outlet *overplay* man, *always* plays *ball-side* or on the side *toward* his teammate defending the ball. He thus prevents the ball from arriving at G.

After 1 and 2 have mastered this idea and technique by alternating positions and locations on the floor, we next add another pair for the three-on-three drill.

In Diagram 320, X with the ball can dribble or feed right to G or left to F. In order to make the defense effective we tell 1 "You will decide for X which way to go." One takes away one choice for X and forces him, for example, to go left. One does this by establishing his position so far to X's right that X cannot possibly go right. The best single stunt is a forward left foot by 1. X can easily go left and surely will. How we stop an easy advance is covered shortly under double-team play. Three can now expect action on his side. The plan could be (and is practical) reversed as 1 plays strong on X's left and forces him right to 2.

Double teaming and when to do it

Our basic double-team rule applies to *all* defenses (Regular Up, Regular Down, 94, etc.) and is as follows: "You will double team at any and all times that you can get to the ball man by taking two or fewer steps from your primary position or assignment. If in doubt, always do it and never worry about the consequences and do it completely and very aggressively." In other words, *when* to double team? Any time you can take two or fewer steps and put pressure on the ball. That is the basic double-team rule.

In addition to the basic rule, we offer these few operational guides and we teach them in the two-on-two drill that we use for overplay, Diagram 319, and we teach double teaming at the same time and as part of the overplay techniques. Actually overplay contributes to double teaming. We overplay in order to get double teams.

As the players operate, we want these guides kept in mind: *Do* double team whenever: 1) The ball is within two steps of you, 2) An opponent drives toward you out of control or without respect for you, 3) You can approach the ball unknown to the ball man (sneak up on the ball, usually from the rear), 4) Opponents cross over each other in lateral moves, Diagram 321. One would jump switch as 2 "sheep dogs" or applies pressure from the rear.

When applying the double team, the two defenders should not get closer than about 12 inches to the opponent, and they should remain erect at the waist. They should not reach in except with short, careful thrusts. They should stay about 60 degrees apart, that is, they should not both be on the same quarter or side of

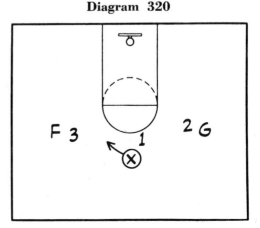

Diagram 319   **Diagram 320**

OVERPLAY DRILL

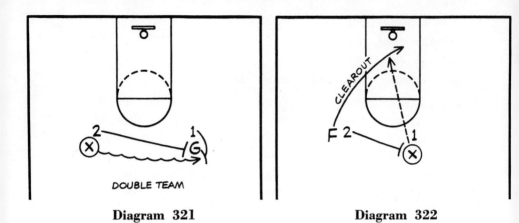

DOUBLE TEAM

Diagram 321   Diagram 322

the opponent, but rather should squeeze him from at least a 60 degree wedge. Normally, the defenders should keep hands high, which obstructs their opponents' vision and encourages their attempted outlet passes to be high. If the defense can force a high pass, the ball stays in the air longer and other defenders have a much better chance to intercept or deflect it toward the other basket.

Double teamers should not allow bounce passes either of course, but these are less apt to occur. The bullet passes must not be allowed because one offensive man is free any time a double team is in effect and bullet passes will wreck the press effect.

Double teaming and when not to do it

1) The ball has to come to you, you do not go to the ball, except as in the third case, stated above. It helps to describe that "the double-team effect must come to you, you do not take the double team to the opponent" except within the two step limit. 2) The double team must not be *later,* i.e., after your man has cleared out in the opposite direction or to the basket, or the ball will be passed to your open man *before* you can apply the double team, Diagram 322.

Number 2 must be alert to F's action, and if F goes early 2 must go with F instead of the ball. The only way to learn which to do is for 2 (and all players) to get a lot of practice in this drill. It can be expanded to a three-on-three drill for advanced skill development.

Intercepting and support of double teams

As the ball force man (1 man in Diagrams 319 and 320) invites X to go to the open side, the coach may fear that X can go freely

162

all the way and escape the defense completely. Number 1 must harass the dribbler from the rear and cause two things to occur: a) 1 must not allow X to go directly at the basket, Diagram 323, but must force him to run a bow route at least two steps off line, Diagram 324, and b) 1 must force him to go somewhat fast and recklessly so that 2 can step over and apply a positive stopper roadblock double team. Should X try to stop or reverse back to the right, 1 would tie him up or take the ball, Diagram 325. We refer to this rear side pursuit as "sheep dog" work, the defender is right on the heels of the dribbler. This force man should at-

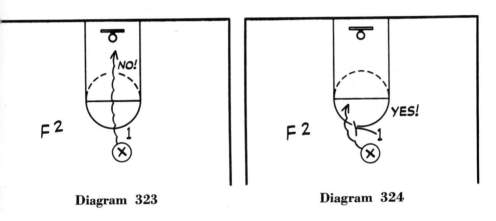

Diagram 323   Diagram 324

tempt to flip the ball loose by the use of a short jab flick from the rear as the ball is out of the dribbler's hand and near the floor. Trying to flick the ball at any other time invites the official to call a hacking foul. The ball should be popped up into the air so that 2 or another alert teammate can intercept. The elbow should be kept in close to the belt and the motion should be upward with open palms, thumbs outward. Do not permit a full arm extension or long reach as this causes loss of balance and fouls.

Rotating and compensating for overplay

As the force man causes movement into a double team, the other three men must be reading the total action and keep in mind the probable reactions of the enemy. If the double team should fail, the remaining three defensive men now play the primary role. They must constantly be asking themselves "To whom or to where is the ball most apt to go next?" The nearest man, the open man,

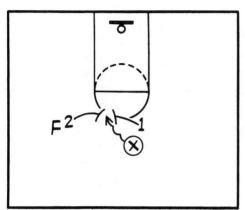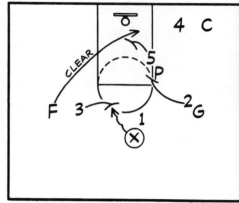

| Diagram 325 | Diagram 326 |

the basket area are prime possibilities. In Diagram 326, should F clear as 3 attempted a double team which failed, 5 would need to compensate to F (who is more dangerous now than is 5's own man P) and 2 would have to "drift" to cover P at the post, thus leaving G open rather than P, C in the corner or F going under, Diagram 326. We call this compensation "drifting" and it may involve one, two or all three of the men not involved in the initial action. Coaches can in this way impress upon their teams that double teaming is a *five*-man action, not a two-man stunt. It helps motivate the "drifters" if they are told and shown that they may well get more interceptions and loose balls and subsequently score easy lay-ups than do the (harder-working) double-team men! This drifting action is the pay off to good front line pressure. It may, of course, result in all five men switching men.

The double-team men may be going down court as the drifters intercept and feed them as the reward for the hustle.

In summary, we play 94 at full court, 2/3, or 1/2 court. The 94 defense is in effect a Regular Up *plus* overplay and double teams. We merely call "94" and point to the floor location at which we begin the front line of resistance.

In 94, we always play the ball very tight on the feed in from out of bounds. The ball defender gets up close to the out of bounds man, holds hands high and moves them rapidly in an attempt to cause a wild throw at best or at least a high lob pass which we have a chance to intercept.

164

THIRTEEN

Augmenting the Man-to-Man Press with Some Zone Principles

Advantages over 94

The addition of a few zone principles gives an entirely different look and a considerably different effect to 94. Advantages are: 1) less tiring, 2) less need for individual match-ups in speed, height and general skill, 3) forces offense to use ball-advance tactics which differ from those required to beat the man-to-man press 94, 4) the best way to teach your own team to operate offensively versus a zone press is to have one of your own and use it in practice.

Disadvantages

The zone-type press is inferior to the man-to-man in these respects: 1) it requires more *team* (unit) drill to perfect; 2) it allows or provides for certain players to rest or loaf at times—both offensive players (which is *bad*, and defensive players (*possibly good!*); 3) it is quite popular as a defense and most coaches have a fairly adequate antidote for it.

X or full court zone press

When we started coaching many years ago we labeled our zone attack with letters from the front of the alphabet (A, B, C, D, etc.) and always have used letters from the bottom of the alphabet for zone defenses. "X" is a signal easily flashed from the bench with 2 crossed fingers and is therefore employed to describe this defense.

PRINCIPLES

This defense differs little from the popular conceptions of zone presses. One principle is that it must be governed by definite rules of action. A second principle is that these rules be simple and easily remembered in the heat of battle. A third principle is that these rules be few in number. The fourth principle is that these rules be universally effective versus most or all offensive tactics.

We align X by assigning imaginary areas of the court to each player, Diagram 327. The total coverage features some overlapping of coverage, but confusion is held to a minimum by the operational rules.

These are the operational rules and coverage assignments:

M or middle man, Diagram 328, operates generally in the area bounded by lines connecting the far free throw circle top to the near corners. M's job is: 1) *chase* the ball once it is fed inbounds. (Yours is the one exception to the double-team rule of *not* going *to* a double team). Force the ball to a wingman, do *not* allow the ball to move down the court center. Keep the ball off-center! 2) Once the ball is in bounds, do not permit a low cross-cut pass. If you anticipate this pass, try to intercept it. 3) You are to go help both wing men double team, but they seldom help you. 4) If the ball gets beyond (past) you, pursue it at sprint speed and apply severe pressure.

Wingman or W will, with one exception, be either on the ball-side or the back side, because the ball will usually not remain in court center. The floor coverage for W is that area to his side of a line drawn from mid-baseline to the sideline-timeline junction, Diagram 329.

If the ball is on *your* side, your assignments are: 1) do not allow the short lob behind you into the rear part of your area. If there are two men in your area, one up front near the baseline and one back near the timeline, allow the feed into the front one but not the back one. 2) Once the ball is in your area, don't allow it to be driven down the sideline. Seal the sideline and expect M to double team from the inside.

If the ball is on the *opposite* side your assignments are different and your coverage line changes, Diagram 330. 1) Do not allow a lob pass back into your corner once the ball has been inbounds on the opposite side. 2) Retreat and cover the deepest man in your area if there are two; if there is *none*, then 3) "Drift" to the center and stay ball-side on any cutter who leaves your initial area and goes toward center court (you are now becoming a replacement for Rover who is busy elsewhere). Diagram 330 shows your area widening to the center.

Rover or the short post man, R: Your area is basically a large

Diagram 327   **Diagram 328**

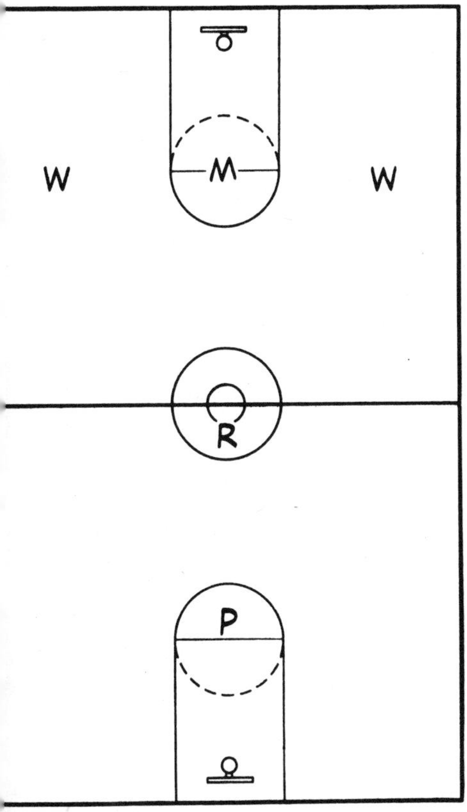

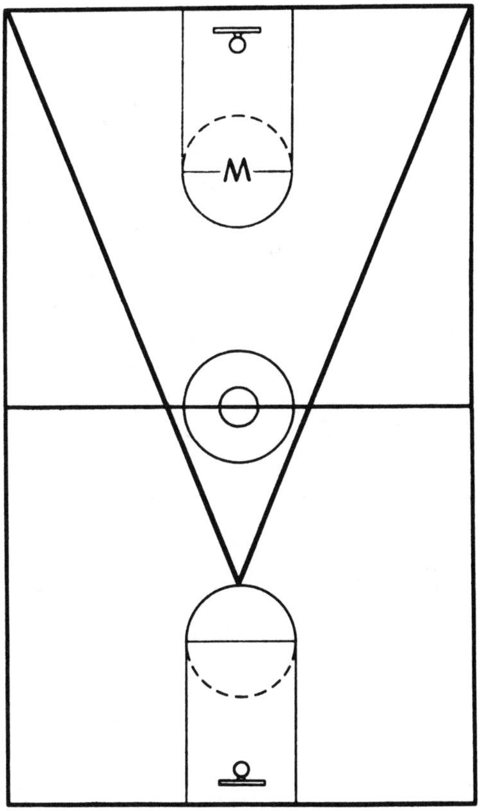

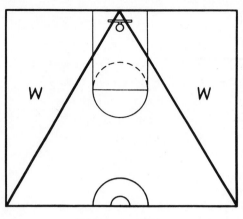

Diagram 329

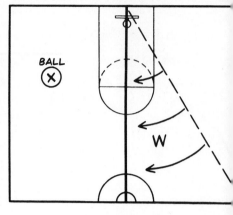

Diagram 330

circle from sideline to sideline concentric with the center jump circle, Diagram 331.

You are primarily a roving trouble-shooter with considerable freedom so that you can capitalize on any offensive error caused by the pressure of the front three defenders. 1) Intercept all passes to a short post man near center court by playing man-to-man and ball-side of any such opponent. If there are two such men, split the difference if they are less than half the width of the floor apart. (If they are farther apart, the far W or P will cover one.) 2) Stop the pass or dribble down the sideline. You always play ball, or strong, side.

P or long post: Your coverage area is usually best described by the curved lines from center circle to each deep corner of the offensive end, Diagram 332. 1) Protect the basket if an opponent is near it. 2) Play on top of all postmen. 3) You can defend two deep men if they are not more than 1/2 court width (25 feet) apart, or 4) Call weakside W back to help you if Rover is engaged on a man; or call Rover back to help if both corners are filled and the ball stays approximately near the middle of the court.

ADJUSTMENTS TO USUAL OFFENSIVE MOVEMENTS

Application of the X action rules would show the defense adjusting versus a typical attack in Diagram 333 which develops into the situation shown in Diagram 334. Rover has responsibility to intercept the pass to the sideline cutting G or to stop the feed down to the centerline forward.

Another typical advance is shown in Diagram 335. Should the

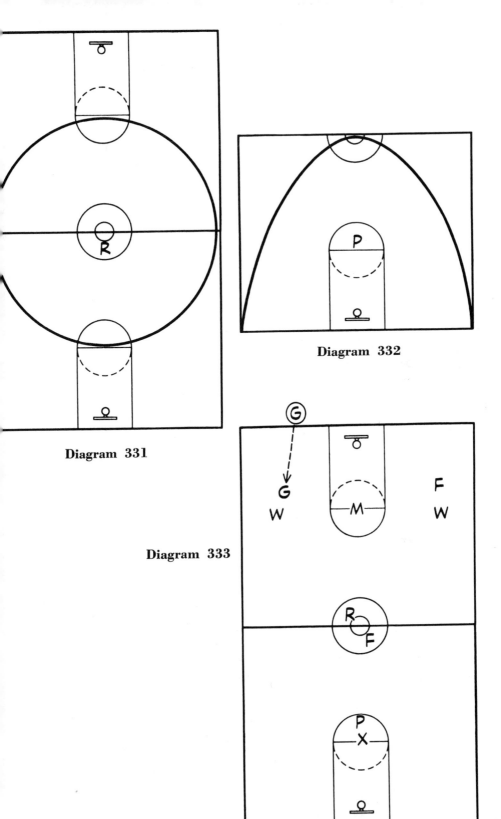

Diagram 331

Diagram 332

Diagram 333

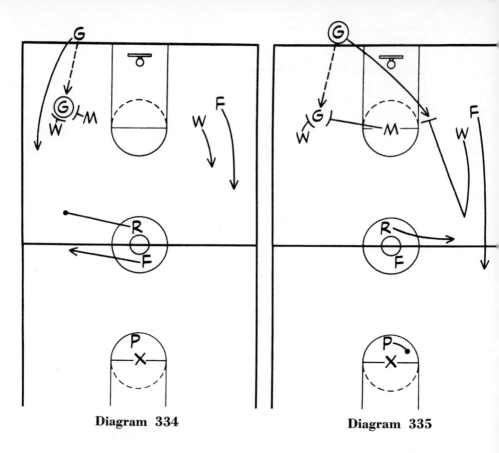

Diagram 334   Diagram 335

timeline forward break to the left side, Diagram 336, Rover can go left also and leave the right sideline cutter F to P if he is fed with a long diagonal pass. In this situation Rover has the *choice* of staying ball-side (which is *left* here) or going strongside (right). Strongside is determined here by the direction of the cut of the in-feed G. This is a good key for Rover.

ADJUSTMENTS TO UNUSUAL MOVES

A couple of examples follow for purposes of proving the validity of the operational rules. In Diagram 337, P must cover and move *while* the ball is in *the air*. In Diagram 338, the right wing must first respect the cross court cutting forward, then return home to seal the sideline cut of the in-feed guard as Rover assumes partial coverage of the crossing forward.

CHANGING AT 1/3 COURT

If the offense penetrates beyond our front three men, we scramble back to 1/3 court and immediately go into our basic Regular Down defense. We seldom stay in X if we don't get a double team

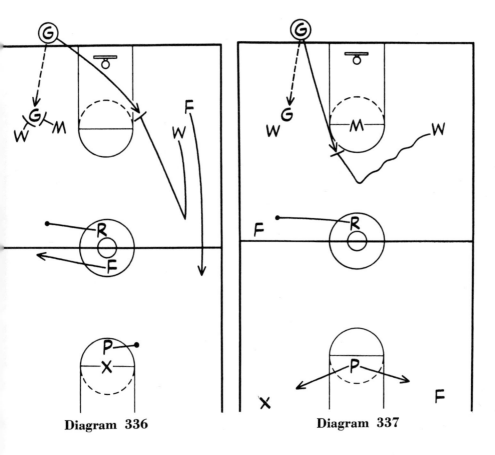

Diagram 336   **Diagram 337**

or an interception after the first three moves of the ball. In reality we play X in front court and Regular Down in the back (opponent's goal) end. Sometimes we change from X to Regular Up.

"Y" or 2/3 court press

We often use, especially later in the year a variation of X which for some reason(s) is more effective versus some teams than is X. We begin to apply the pressure about two strides in front of the time line, Diagram 339.

SIMILARITIES AND DIFFERENCES COMPARED TO X

Y is similar to X basically and little new learning is involved. The main differences are in the time span from in-feed to pressure application, and in the different location from which the defenders attack the offense.

ADVANTAGES

Setting up twenty feet farther back than we do in X allows us

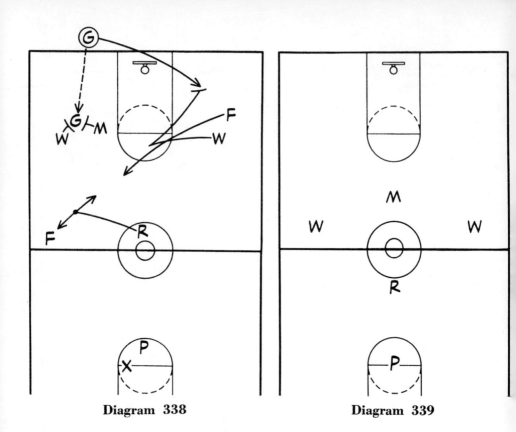

Diagram 338   **Diagram 339**

a couple more seconds to catch our breath, gives us more time to get organized and properly aligned, and gives us less territory to cover. We thus can usually effect a better coverage because of our relative closeness to each other. The periphery of this defense is smaller, hence the core is more solid and more difficult to penetrate.

DISADVANTAGES

We give up about twenty linear feet of floor length, therefore the offense is closer to pay dirt should our defense fail. If the opponent is able to pass accurately into these restricted areas and cut effectively, this defense is lacking. If the offense can move the ball two quick times and avoid our first or second double team, we are out of Y and needful of a change.

CHANGING AT 1/3 COURT

As in X, we quickly scramble out of Y into Regular Down or Regular Up, whichever was predetermined, if we cannot hold the ball in front of our front three men.

172

"Z" or scrambling at 1/3 court

If our change back to Regular defense from Y is not effective, we often *stay in* the transition or "scramble" tactics. Essentially we are jamming back to about the top of the circle and trying to make X coverage work from there. This is essentially a spearhead zone and our main objective is to move fast and furiously with *no* zone coverage assignment except trying to anticipate where we might be of trouble to the offense. Everyone is free to slide and "drift" with *overplay, double team,* and *intercept* on his mind. It is a good tactic for this reason alone—no strings or responsibilities attached, just pride and an appetite for the ball.

This Z or "scramble" as we call it is apt to develop spontaneously into Regular Up as the boys resort to the most natural of their defensive tendencies, find a man and overplay him. I repeat that there are no assignments in Z, it is a free lance deal all the way, the only such defense we ever employ!

FOURTEEN

A Combination Defense

Advantages

For years we have sought a solution to the need of a defense with the simplicity of the zone plus the values of a man-to-man. It has seemed that the logical starting point would be with a zone alignment and then establish rules or guidelines which direct movements of defensive players that would have man-to-man effect. If such rules can be developed that are comprehensive enough to cover all offensive threats yet few and simple enough to be easily understood by the players, a very good defense should result.

The "option" (each man has approximately four defensive options which he applies sequentially) or "rule" (each man is guided by his own individual defensive rules) defense presented here is the result of personal experimentation toward development of such a defense. Surely it is not foolproof and surely other coaches have individually and collectively striven for the same objective. My own efforts were bolstered considerably when a lecture by Milton Jowers of South-West Texas State revealed what he had been doing with considerable success and many of his conceptions permeate this scheme.

The best zone, in our opinion is the 1-3-1, and the best man-to-man defense is a sink. By combining these two basics, we get what we call "F-44," (F for Frostburg, and 44 because there are four sets of rules for four different positions).

174

Weaknesses

There are a few weak spots in the F-44 defense. 1) The corners can be exploited if a team has *two* good corner shooters. 2) The flank areas have a soft spot which we call the 1-4 gap. 3) The core of this defense is weak if once penetrated. 4) Certain overload combinations strain it.

Alignment

The reader should keep in mind that F-44 is considered to be primarily a man-to-man defense even though it appears to be a zone. This implies that basic man-to-man rules apply at all times unless a F-44 rule contradicts it. We insist on Regular defense techniques at all times and all these man-to-man skills must prevail as implied rules.

Each man's position is clearly defined by imaginary lines on the floor and the operational rules are listed in rank order of application.

Assignments and rules for coverage

Number I, the Back Man (should be big and willing to run).

Your coverage is from the baseline out 13 feet (to the low edge or broken half of the near jump circle) and sideline to sideline, Diagram 340.

RULES FOR I: 1) Protect baseline (basic Regular defense rule). 2) Play on top of all low posts, whether you are stationary on them or moving past them on the run (basic Regular defense rule). 3) Any dribblers forced or encouraged to enter your area must be greeted with a solid jump switch type stance and stopped dead *as they enter*. 4) Move while the ball is airborne so that you arrive not later than the ball on all pass attempts into your area (basic Regular-Up overplay rule). 5) Stay *inside* the ball at all times including rebounding.

Number II, the Post Man

Your coverage is the three second lane plus 1/2 step wider on each side, Diagram 341.

RULES FOR II: 1) Versus an offense *with* a post man: Play him man-to-man with overplay and try to prevent him getting the ball

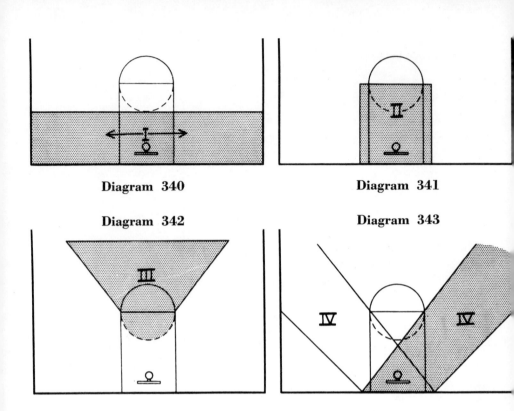

Diagram 340

Diagram 341

Diagram 342

Diagram 343

(basic man-to-man rule). If he does get the ball, play him extremely close and consider him a shooter even though he may be a screener, feeder, or decoy. Your defensive mates are responsible for him if he drives past you. 2) Versus an offense with *no* post man: a. play a one-man zone in the middle of your area, b. if there are two men in I's area, go cover the second one man-to-man c. should a post man enter your area *late* come home immediately *or* prearrange with III or IV to cover this situation.

Number III, the Point Man (must be a hustler).

Your area is the complete circle plus the center front court bounded by lines from the circle free throw junction toward the timeline-sideline junction, 2 1/2 strides above the circle, Diagram 342.

RULES FOR III: 1) *Never* allow the ball to stay centered in your area, force it right or left to IV or to the extreme corners of your area. 2) Once forced off-center, exert ball-side overplay coverage on any middle or offside guard so that ball cannot return to center or beyond unless it goes nearer the timeline. 3) As ball is on a side, do not allow empty men from your area to cut down the

176

lane or near side of the lane. Play ball-side all the way down to the low limit of your area (basic Regular Cutter rule). 4) Do not allow any driver to penetrate between you and IV. This III-IV gap is a critical area and if the ball gets through this seam into the heart of this defense, the damage is great. 5) Rebound at the key top.

IV, the Flank Men (there are two, left and right)

Your coverage area is bounded by two lines. One is a diagonal from the near junction of the free throw line and circle to the opposite far corner of number II's area. The other is one approximately parallel to the first, and is from the near lane and baseline junction to the near sideline and free throw line (extended) junction, Diagram 343.

RULES FOR IV WHEN BALL IS ON YOUR SIDE OF FLOOR: 1) Don't allow ball to go down *your* area toward basket (force it to either III's area or I's area. Stay *inside* it, do not get ahead of dribbler as he may reverse and go down your lane. Encourage him to go into the corner where I will be waiting with the road block. 2) If dribbler is forced into corner, don't try to keep him there, but retreat and overplay on anyone else in your area to prevent the ball coming out of the corner. 3) One exception to rule 2 is: sag to overplay on outstanding post man if II needs help and thus allow the out-feed from the corner. 4) Protect the III-IV seam. 5) Try to cover the I-IV soft spot if a long range shooter has continued success there.

RULES FOR IV WHEN BALL IS ON OPPOSITE SIDE: 1) Drift down to the lowest limit of your area and protect the hoop by overplaying on any low post men in your area. 2) If there are no low post men in the low limits of your area, be alert for all weakside cutters coming toward basket.

The entire defense appears as shown in Diagram 344.

Teaching and learning the F-44 defense

We cover this plan in a classroom session for about twenty minutes and quickly cover each man's rules. We give each man a couple of sheets describing the defense.

After practicing this defense for about 10 minutes daily for three days, we seldom if ever give it more physical practice time. About once weekly we ask each man to quickly recite his coverage

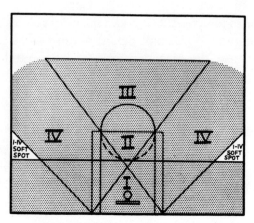

Diagram 344

rules and always employ our man-to-man defenses in practice. We find that F-44 is usually ready when we need it without costing us any practice time.

One main strength is its zone appearance, but most zone attacks are ineffective.

Another main strength is its simplicity and solid coverage. I like it.

FIFTEEN

Transition from Defense

Back to Offense

One of the five general situations in basketball is that time period, usually brief but always sudden and often unexpectedly abrupt in occurrence, the transition from defense to offense.

The important thing is the necessity of changing mood or attitude of the defense—he must instantly *think* offense instead of defense; he must instantly advance rather than retreat (go north instead of south) and subsequently establish a continued offensive game. This game can perhaps be a fast break, then a continuity pattern as described initially in these pages.

Defensive rebounding

The basis for any change from defense to offense is gaining control of the ball. In addition to interceptions, steals, and being granted the ball after a score, the rebounding is most responsible for ball control. This discussion of transition from defense to offense shall be concentrated on beginning with defensive rebounding and fast breaking to the far end.

In the previous discussion of rebounding, the major points have been mentioned. We do not give credit to a defensive rebounder for a rebound until he has successfully moved the ball away from the board. If by a pass, before his second step (no dribble allowed if possible) and if by a drive, it must be immediate and fast.

Aggression, "Go! Go! Go!"

I see one simple need to be aggressive with the ball in transition from defense—safety. To come too deliberately seems to invite trouble. Perhaps we will not commit as many errors ourselves but the opponents simply have too much opportunity to plan devastation for us. The more aggressive our transition is, the less chance the opposition has to retaliate.

In addition to this safety or self-preservation concept, an aggressive attitude, expressed overtly by voice, action, and deed seems beyond any doubt to instill a certain "head of steam" in our game which tends to carry us beyond our normal limits of performance—it picks up our spirit and makes us better perhaps than we would otherwise tend to be.

Third, it's fun and "You can't beat fun!"

From five-man cup to fast break

In the course of any game or for that matter, any practice, we tend to get almost any and every possible origin for our fast break. We try to realize that we can and will fast break any time we can and that we can fast break from the following situations: 1) successful field goal by opponents, 2) unsuccessful field goal by opponents that we rebound, 3) successful free throw by opponents, 4) unsuccessful free throw by opponents that we rebound, 5) interception, 6) retrieved loose ball, 7) possession from jump ball, 8) granted possession after violation.

Most of our learning drill is centered around the five-man cup that we hopefully will establish at each field goal attempt by our opponent. This five-man cup was discussed earlier under Regular Down defense.

Various types of fast break

There are a couple of classic popular fast break patterns. One is the three-lane with the ball coming down the center lane being passed from lane to lane with little or no dribbling. Another is similar but the ball advances down a side lane with the dribble. There are other variations of these two plans. There are also the unorganized fast breaks.

Johnny McLendon of Kentucky State seems to have most of the answers about the fast break game.[1] His success record is no doubt due to his intelligence, his complete dedication to the game and his sincere concern for each individual player.

My favorite break pattern

I prefer a two-lane fast break, a center lane and one side lane. I drill my boys in a three-lane pattern and to this day have never dared suggest that one of the side lane sprinters are going along as a decoy. If anything else is different or unique about my fast break it is the initial outlet from the board—I like to bring the ball by the most simple and direct route, the drive by the rebounder himself right up the "gut." That should not be possible against most defenses, but I find that it is! The third rather significant belief I hold is that the speed of advance of the ball is less critical than the speed of the front runner. These ideas are discussed below.

Highly organized—but not much!

I suspect that the first-time fan would see little organization to our type of fast break. I'm also sure our players consider it just the opposite. We have only one fast break scheme and it will develop in either one of two ways. The first choice is shown in Diagram 345. Whoever gets the ball off the board fills the middle lane. The second choice is shown by example in Diagram 346 and differs from choice one only in that the outlet is a pass out to some free player who becomes the middle man. We always attempt to go choice one and use choice two only as an alternate.

Outletting

For the first choice pattern, the rebounder employs the spread-eagle technique as described earlier in offensive drills. He pivots without dribbling and faces down-court in a low, hard turn exactly as he does on the first move of the wheeling drill. If he can see

---

[1] John McLendon, *Fast Break Basketball: Fundamentals and Fine Points.* Parker Publishing Co., Inc., 1965.

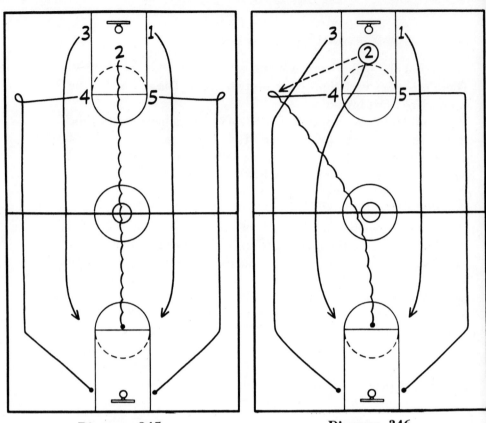

Diagram 345   **Diagram 346**

the floor (unobstructed, meaning no one is there) he can drop
the ball down in a hard bounce and drive off low and hard up-
court. He should now become alert for anyone looming up in his
path. Should danger appear he must not approach any closer than
1 1/2 strides unless he can stop, feed off or circumnavigate this
danger; he must be under control. If this driver looks ahead, he
is usually able to drive past any stationary defender.

We insist that this ball carrier go through the center circle since
he must stay in the center of the court for the last half of the
trip. If he is forced off center he is unable to feed to the far side
with complete safety. He stops at the free throw line if there is
any defender in line with the basket. He then feeds either side
man, who by now should be in position near the board corner, or
he should take the two-point free throw from the line.

It is the rebounder who is the outlet man and he becomes the
ball carrier in the first choice fast break.

In the second choice pattern, the rebounder cannot pivot
(wheel) and see a clear floor, he looks to the right sideline for a

182

clearing guard (unless the rebound is by number 1 in Diagram 346, in which case the outlet is to the left).

We prefer and drill the use of the hook pass to these clearing guards because less wind-up is required than for a baseball pass and it is higher than a chest pass.

If the defense is normal, the outlet feed should hit the clearing guard at about the free throw line extended and about 3 to 6 feet from the sideline. If the opponents pressure either the re-bounder or the clearing guard, the guard may have to expect the feed one stride nearer the baseline. If the defense is lax, he can start up the sideline and might be fed a step above the free throw line.

When to Feed

The rebounder should feed before his second foot hits the deck if possible, or before he has need to dribble. Practice on this.

Guard Clearing: Where, Why, How

Both guards should break laterally out on the extended free throw line and perpendicular to the sideline. They will tend to round the corner; this is permissible for the weakside guard as he will probably not receive the feed, but the outlet guard will have his back to the ball too long as he makes a rounded turn and the feeder cannot possibly feed him properly. Train the clearing guards to turn 3/4 (clockwise for a right guard) and temporarily face their own baseline. This is unnatural but best.

The weakside guard is the most important man from here on in. He must sprint, staying within 3 feet of the sideline until he hits the far free throw line extended, then break sharply to the near board corner and *stop* and stay. Flank speed. He will go at least one dozen times for every time he gets the ball but his job is to pull any deep defender back and out of the face of the com-ing ball carrier! Should this defender not retreat *then* the first clearing guard can be fed. He must: 1) Stay near the sideline, else he puts himself in the hip pocket of the deep defender and covers himself. 2) Sprint. 3) Be willing to go time after time after time at sprint speed. 4) Not cross through the lane (go fast, then stand and loaf!).

Give the clearing guard the long bomb (as described in offen-sive drills) whenever possible.

The Ball Carrier

The actions of the ball carrier, described before can be summed up thus: 1) Stay under control and never drive into defensive trouble. 2) Be in center court by the time you hit the time line. 3) Be under control and ready to stop when you reach the free throw circle. Teammates are responsible for warning you of defensive pressure from the rear. You cannot, under any circumstance, charge as you come down. 4) Most important is that you *do arrive*, even if a little late. Do not come so fast that control suffers. The most important thing on *this* fast break is *not* how fast the ball comes, but how fast the clearing guard gets down!

Third Man

The third man is any one of the remaining three who can get into the strongside sideline lane. It may be the rebounder, or the near or far board (rebound triangle) man. Whoever he is, he crosses over either ahead of or behind the ball carrier, but remembers that the ball carrier has the right of way. His action rule is the same as the first or clearing guard: close to sideline, sprint speed, change course when, and not before, he reaches the free throw line extended, fast to the near board corner and stop.

The Two Trailers

The last two men, whoever they are, should fill the running lanes on either side of court center and come quickly and fast. They are free to go and help wherever they think they can be effective—but we want them there no later than three or four strides behind the ball.

The Good Shot Rules Still Prevail

I really don't care what shot we take after we arrive but I do insist that we have worked too hard and too long to give up the basketball unless it falls through the strings! Five men have run a total of about 450 feet at full speed, we have worked hard at defense for some time, rebounded hard, etc. "It didn't come easy, boys, and it's not going easy!" Remember the good shot rules and if all of them prevail, bang it in!

Phasing Into Pattern

As soon as it seems that the advantages, if any, of the fast break no longer exist, phase into Trample or whatever offense we're using. Don't waste time hoping a defender dies of old age so you can get an unearned bucket.

In conclusion, this fast break may not look effective nor highly organized. We believe it is optimally both.

If any coach begins to stress fast break, it may be some consolation for him to realize that a good fast break requires about one full year (12 months) to develop if you have boys who are not fast break trained and experienced. It seems to mature over the summer by virtue of mental practice only.

You need to *think* fast break every time but it won't always occur. Do not force it if the opportunity doesn't exist. If you install a fast break in November it will be at its best next October if *all* the players don't graduate, at least this has been true in my experience.

This fast break described here may not be very "fast" at times, but teams of *any* speed can use it to advantage. No team is too slow to break this way.

Get! GET! GET!

Part III

Special Situation Offenses and Defenses

SIXTEEN

Keep-Away Game

There are at least two general theories on "freezing" the ball, i.e., playing "keep away." We prefer the latter term as it more completely defines intent. One theory is that the keep-away plan be a definite game of its own. The other idea is that the keep-away game should be the basic offense in disguise.

We do in some situations use the Trample to freeze the ball but we also have a genuine keep-away game which is more reliable at times.

Identifying the defense

The technique of playing keep away is somewhat affected by the type of defense exerted by the opponents. If the defensive pressure is man-to-man, we need to move with drives and cuts. If the pressure is zone, we will move the ball but restrict the cutting and driving.

The most critical aspect of this problem is determining whether the pressure is man-to-man or zone. As far as we are concerned there is one and only one way to determine whether we are being pressured man-to-man or zone. The answer is so simple it may insult the intellect but it amounts to merely observing to see how many defenders attack the man with the ball. If one man attacks, it is man-to-man, if two or more, it is zone. Let all other maneuvers, clues, actions be ignored. If there is no pressure at all, consider it zone—it's easier that way.

Uses

1) *Stall:* Obviously if we want to protect a lead, the keep-away game is useful. 2) *Rest:* There may be times, indeed there have been times with squads of fewer than ten men when, with a lead, we have nearly run out of steam, perhaps as early as the end of the third quarter. Going into a keep-away game for about two minutes has allowed us to: a. catch our breath, b. aggravate the opponents and cool down their hot streak without using a time out (the clock continues to run during a stall!), c. on a few precious occasions when we were losing a lead we have played keep away in order to *rest* only to have the opponents panic and we pick up as many as six easy lay-ups in two minutes. They sometimes create so much fun for you that you refuse to rest even when you need to! 3) *Force out of zone:* As we consider it more of a man's game to play versus man-to-man defenses, we find that if we can get an early lead on a zone team, we can play keep away and often force the zone to move out and take us on man-to-man. We are usually assured that the man-to-man which ensues is inferior to their zone, otherwise the zone would not have been employed initially.

Freezing the ball with regular offensive pattern

One technique is to use the regular pattern, Trample for example, and only *appear* to attempt penetration to the basket. It is usually best to set up the pattern about one step farther out than usual and run screens, cuts, to look in but fail to take the ball inside the defensive perimeter. The pattern should continue with all normal movement and the ball should not be kept stationary lest the opponents soon realize the offense is merely feigning an honest attack. Several precious minutes can easily slip by as one employs this idea of running the normal pattern about one step deeper than usual and only "trying" but never releasing team control!

Freezing the ball versus zone pressure

If we determine the defense to be zone, we play "Zebra" (Z for zone) attack. We align as shown in Diagram 347. We merely follow a few simple rules because we know if there are two men

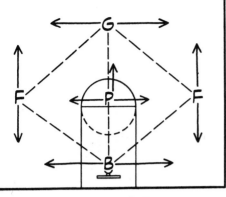

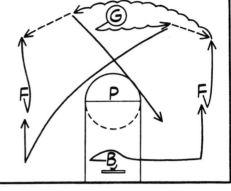

| Diagram 347 | Diagram 348 |

attacking the ball, one of us is free somewhere on the floor; so we align in this manner to stay dispersed and feed the open man.

Zebra rules: 1) Stay dispersed. 2) Move the ball to the free man *before* defense arrives on the ball man. 3) If no pressure, stand and hold the ball, do *not* dribble it if there is no pressure on you. 4) You may need to dribble occasionally in order to maintain control, but not unless necessary. 5) Be alert to free cuts for the *unmolested* lay-up. Go for these if you can get a drive or feed a teammate for the unmolested lay-up. 6) Stay out of the corners and at least six feet from the timeline.

Freezing the ball versus man-to-man pressure

In past years we would set up a two-guard offense versus the man-to-man but we now find a variation of Zebra is equally effective so we need not install another pattern, Diagram 348.

G fakes one way and dribbles the other (left here) and does not turn his back to the basket as he does so. As he dribbles left, the left sideline forward fakes down, then comes back to the ball and is fed. G then cuts through to the opposite corner as the opposite forward comes up to ultimately accept the feed from the ball forward who dribbles across court (becomes the new guard). This replacement guard then feeds the opposite forward and cuts to the far (on his own original side) corner. In the meantime the baserunner has filled in that side.

This game, which we call the "Monkey" game (M for man-to-man attack) is then a game of four-man dribbling, feeding, and cutting away around a high post. It is a continuity and does not need a re-set if interrupted.

SEVENTEEN

Advancing Versus the Press

The essence of any press is its ability to prevent the offense from advancing the ball downcourt. Obviously the offensive plans must include some scheme to counteract this threat but there are a good many teams who display little organization in this regard. This complete trust to fate is not my dish. The lack of organization in this department is a positive means of suicide which will be immediately apparent to all fans, all opponents and to the score keeper. Death will not only be imminent, it will be quick and hideous!

Advancing versus the zone press

An advance used to attack a zone press needs to be exact and cocksure. Excellent ball handlers may need little organization but teams of lesser talent need, it seems to me, some rather comprehensive guidelines to follow. There are many zone press advances and they vary according to the zone encountered. The basic viewpoint which many young coaches may overlook is that a zone press is basically a zone defense and should be treated much like a normal non-press zone.

Use of zone principles

As the zone press is considered to be basically the same as any other zone, the following guidelines might apply: 1) stay dispersed, 2) don't dribble too much, 3) hunt for holes and move the ball by passing, 4) do not hurry—most players do not realize just how long ten seconds are—be sure they really know, 5) use cutters; you *can* cut and drive against zones, don't fail to do so when possible.

Our favorite, a seven option play

The advance that has served us best in moving the ball is shown in Diagram 349. It is essentially a long and short post with a little three-man option play exactly like the football split T option running pass involving the quarterback, halfback and weakside end.

The out-of-bounds guard feeds in to the near guard or the forward on the opposite side. The example in Diagram 349 will be to the right guard. Both sideline men first drive downcourt two steps (if pressured) and come back to receive the feed. The recipient wheels and tries to drive downcourt as his first option. If stopped by a single or double team, he looks next for the short post S as S moves first downcourt for the long lead feed and if not fed, comes to the ball-side of the court for option two. If option two is not possible, G looks next crosscourt to F who is clearing down the far sideline about three or four steps ahead of the ball, option three. If no action, lead G pulls up and feeds back to the in-feed G who is trailing the ball carrier about three steps and slightly toward the center of the court, option 4. This trailing G tries first to run at the clearing F as this will put him quickly past the double-team men who threatened the lead guard. This is option 5. If this trailing G is stopped it will be by the defender who *should* be covering clearing F, so G can therefore feed long to F, option 6. Short post S has maintained his location ahead of the ball as has the long post. If this sixth option is plugged, either S or P are open long, option 7. We drill this frequently in early season and it has been adequate.

Advancing versus man-to-man press

Advancing against the zone press is one thing; going downcourt in the face of a good man-to-man deal is something else! Certain similar principles prevail in both situations, certain others are exactly opposite.

Offensive Pressure

The master plan should be based on *offensive* pressure. If they

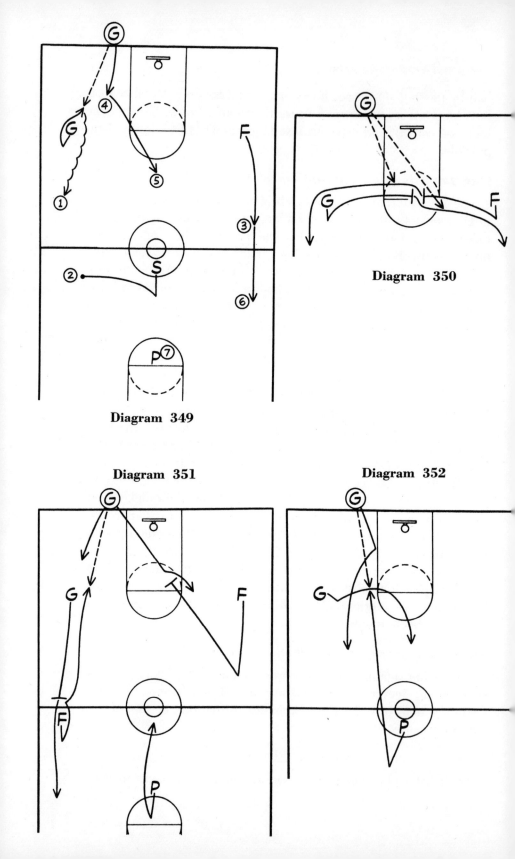

Diagram 350

Diagram 349

Diagram 351

Diagram 352

press us, we'll press our offense at them equally hard. The more aggressively the defense meets the offense, the easier it is to drive the ball past the defense. In other words, don't stand versus the man-to-man press. Every man must *move*.

LATERAL SCREENS

In the zone press advance it is sound to maintain dispersion and to never cross or pass closely to a teammate. This is true because there is little chance of screening a defender as another will be waiting. In the man-to-man attack it is very helpful to screen a teammate. One good deal is shown in Diagram 350. This lateral screen should be a high speed deal and the defensive men are apt to be literally cracked. I have observed at least two legal serious shoulder injuries to defensive players who could not avoid this action. The feed should come one step after teammates emerge from the cross.

VERTICAL INTERCHANGE

If the lateral screens do not serve well, we tend to next look to a vertical interchange near a sideline, shown in Diagram 351. Two men (predetermine who) align near a sideline and on a bounce or slap of the ball, or some other cue, the near man, G, screens F coming up. The in-feed man hits F as he comes to the ball (relatively easily done) and then the feeder G has two options. He may drive past the near F for a return feed or he may cut off the rear screen of the opposite side F for a cross cut feed.

USE OF POST MAN

Post men are always alert for the long feed and should be used if the initial advance plan fails. It is quite easy to send post men down to the far half of the court and then have them reverse and come back into the near court directly at the ball, Diagram 352. It is very difficult for a press to stop an in-feed to a tall man coming directly at the ball. If the guards will cut past this newly established post, the old post-split game is a natural and will usually penetrate a press of either zone or man-to-man design.

The post men can align in tandem, one on either side of the timeline. They can run a vertical interchange with the long post coming to the ball after a screen by the short post who thereafter goes on downcourt for decoy purposes or to receive the long bomb.

Use of the Exceptional Ball Handler

It has been my extreme good fortune on rare occasion to have one man so adept at the drive that the only press advance plan needed was to give him the ball and get away from him! In case this man is injured, ill, or fouled out, one should still have a team advance ready. Having a good team advance also puts more strain on your own team press in practice and causes your press to mature.

EIGHTEEN

Other Aspects of the Game

Jump ball offense

I believe in and use only one jump ball scheme and that is based on defensive consciousness. Some coaches subscribe to the theory that "if we're tall enough to get the tap, we'll get it without complex plays; if we're not tall enough, extended drill is not worthwhile." I agree with this approach. I do not deny the value of obtaining possession of all free balls and quite possibly do not concentrate enough effort to this aspect of the game.

Jump ball defense

1. MATCH UP: We always align on the defensive side of our assigned men on jump balls. We line up on the side nearest the opponent's basket. We will always be defensively sound and there will *always* be two of us adjacent which is an offensive advantage; notice 1 and 2 in Diagram 353. If one of the opposing four non-jumpers is a strong threat, the defender of that person will call for aid from the defensive teammate on the opposite side of this man. In Diagram 353, 4 could slide over a step to aid 2 on his man.

2. LONG FORMATION: If we fear we may lose the tap to either a strong tapper or to good non-jumpers, we go to a long formation for purposes of stopping the fast break from the jump, Diagram 354. It is defensively supreme and if the tap goes long *our* way, we are virtually assured of possession.

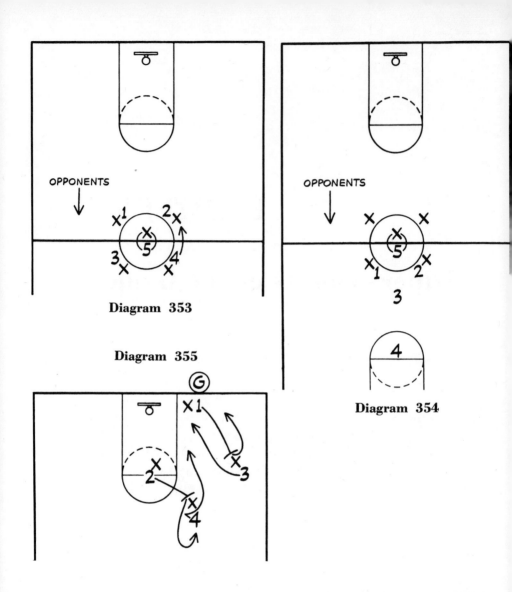

Diagram 353

Diagram 355

Diagram 354

Regardless of which alignment, we ask the men on or near the circle to keep their knees bent and their hands at least chest high because when the tap comes their way, low hands are never quick enough. First consideration is to get the ball the instant it is tapped since the jump restrictions then end. It is always a mistake to expect the ball to come to you—it will never arrive.

Out-of-bounds play

The best set plays in basketball are possible from out-of-bounds situations. The surest single scoring potential in the game is from the out-of-bounds situation under the offensive basket. If I could be given a single opportunity to score within just a few seconds, give my team the ball *out of bounds* under our basket!

Offensive end of court

There seems to be a need for only one good out-of-bounds play for each of two purposes at the offensive end. If scoring is a must, a scoring play is appropriate. Such scoring plays are usually not highly reliable except to provide for the medium distance shot. If you also feel a need for a play with lay-up potential that will, in addition, fairly well insure gaining possession, perhaps a second out-of-bounds play is necessary. We have never been satisfied with one play serving all these requirements and therefore usually have two, one for possession and the lay-up, another for the medium range screen shot.

Possession or scoring?

1. POSSESSION: Our favorite possession play is shown in Diagram 355. At a slap of the ball 1 breaks toward either 2 or 3 and sets a rear screen on their defensive man. Whichever man he does not approach screens for 4. As soon as 1's screen is set, 2 (in this example) breaks either over or under the screen and the screener breaks the opposite way—both come back to the basket. It sounds a little strange, but the *screener* 1 is most often open for a close shot. The man who screens for 4 balances back for defense.

The interesting thing about this play is that after running it a few times, one of the four inbounds men can often break early, before the starting signal, and get an easy lay-up.

The best ball handler or a good tall man should be the feeder.

2. SCORING: We like the four abreast break out pattern in Diagram 356 for the jump shot attempt. It is fairly popular and used by many teams in some form or other. It is relatively foolproof. It can be varied from game to game for consistently good results.

SIDE COURT

We seldom if ever need a side court out-of-bounds play. When we do, the one shown in Diagram 357 is our choice. It gets the ball in and occasionally produces a score on the shot over the screen or a drive left or right.

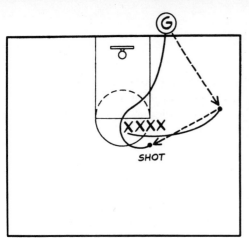

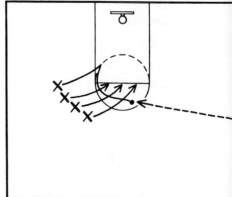

| Diagram 356 | Diagram 357 |

Long End Plays

The long end plays are either the long bomb to a post man or are the normal press advance patterns.

Defensing the Out-of-Bounds Play

We want to mass-up somewhat near the basket and play loose because of the threat of the rear screen. We will give up the outside shot rather than risk a rear pick for the lay-up. We try to be all eyes in all directions and we jam up like quail in a covey so that the offense cannot slip up behind us. We want to be ready early, hands up and especially conscious of the cutter coming to the basket early. If we are behind in the score with time running out, we play Regular Up on all out-of-bounds play with full pressure on the out-of-bounds man; otherwise it is Regular Down and sink more than usual.

The free throw game

The single aspect of basketball coaching which yields the greatest rewards in directly affecting game outcome, with a minimal amount of coaching frustration is free throw shooting. The sad part of this is that few fans, and perhaps coaches also, believe good free throw shooting is anything more than luck or inherent ability—they do not give credit to coaching. I am convinced that it is an aspect which can be positively affected by coaching. I believe some free throw shooters are born, I also believe they can be *made*, i.e., they need not be born with the skill. Does, then, attention to free throw shooting pay off? Yes! How much? Our teams, over the years win up to 30 and 40 percent of *all* the games played by shooting well at the free throw line! Our score books prove it! Many game aspects are inseparably bound to this facet, including playing sound defense and allowing a smaller number of field goals to be made by our opposition as we are fouling fewer times than they, even though we are smaller.

Can win 1/3 of your games

For free throw success we suggest: 1) shoot at least 50 each night in the twenty minutes allotted to individual shooting. 2) Move your feet after each shot. 3) Start the ball slowly, reach far, and with the ball moving faster, release gently. 4) Put the ball up for a vertical descent; gravity makes the point. 5) Mentally challenge the hoop; dare anything or anyone to question your chances of scoring. 6) Several times each night after team workout begins we interrupt our action and each man gets his ball, goes to a basket and shoots ten. After 10 shots, he runs a lap for each one he missed. He rebounds his own and is allowed no warm-ups. We do at least five of these rounds (50 or more) most of them in the last half of practice when we are tired and unsteady 7). Frequently send them to the line and give them only two attempts; if they miss either they run a couple of laps. 8) Ask them to practice free throws mentally (at the dinner table, walking to class, etc.).

I believe they learn not to miss!

Daily Check List of

Offensive and Defensive

Essentials

INDIVIDUAL OFFENSE	INDIVIDUAL DEFENSE
one-on-one keep away	defend low post
wheeling	defend medium post
rocker step	defend high post
drag	guarding baseline
dribbling	defending jump shooter
lob across court	defending set shooter
long pass lob	avoid screens
lay-ups near side	going over screens
cross over lay-up	going through screens: when
lay-ups down the middle	and why
tips on jump shooting	going under screens
shooting over screens	helping
following shot (blocking out)	switching
free throw shooting	rebounding
board shot position and tips	flash posts
outlet feeding	blocking out
tapping	defense on the ball
cutting	cutters
high speed lay-ups	learn defense in head, feet then
setting screens	hands
jockey	play corner shooter

INDIVIDUAL OFFENSE

rebounding (spread-eagle drill)
jump balls
where, high, medium, and low
  posts play
when to shoot
baseline drive
trailers for lay-ups
position on free throws
one-on-one trying to score
how to flash post
advancing versus man-to-man
  press
advancing versus zone press

INDIVIDUAL DEFENSE

sinking
overplaying
post split
getting lost
facing
free throw positioning
pointing
head up
tail down
fast feet
weight on heels not toes
talk to buddies
how to draw charging foul

TEAM OFFENSE

jump ball plays
in-bounds plays (side and end-
  line)
patterns against man-to-man
patterns against zones (all
  types)
fast break
rebounding balance cup
playing in pressure situations
  (overtime)
how to adjust to switching defenses (zone to man-to-man
  and back)
how to play against half court
  press
how to screen (double and
  triple)
post split
give-go

TEAM DEFENSE

jump ball
man-to-man defense
be familiar with zones
overplay
double teaming
man-to-man press
zone press
half court press
3/4 court press
rebounding cup
defense of in-bounds plays
defense of screen game
defense of weave game
how to get ball from a team
  freezing
defense against pattern team
defense against free lance team
how to defend in last seconds
  of game (close)

TEAM OFFENSE

freeze game against man-to-
   man
freeze game against zone
rebounding missed free throws
hunt for holes against zone
work for last shot (how)
discipline to run pattern
how to rotate to rebounding
   position

TEAM DEFENSE

defense in overtime
how to adjust to fast break
   team
how to adjust to good post man
how to adjust to good long
   shooter
how to defend unusual offenses
pursuing
collapsing

Index